"As a golfer, a father, and a believer, this account is one I could not put down. You cannot get away from the specialness of this book. This is the essence of what faith looks like this side of heaven. This is the essence of what faith looks like in the midst of the most trying of circumstances. I wish I would have known David. I look forward to meeting him in heaven."

- **Bill Rogers**, 1981 – PGA Player of the Year, British Open Champion

"Few books have captivated me like Laura Gilbert's *Journey To The Dance*. With the turning of each page, your heart will race and tears will flow as you witness a family's greatest battle and how their enduring faith never wavered.

As one who lost a wife to cancer, I could barely read some pages. But read on because the same book will cause you to rejoice enthusiastically! You will rejoice over a family who refused to give up. You will rejoice over glimpses of God's grace---a nurse experiencing the presence of angels in David's hospital room; a physician quietly reciting scripture while his young patient fights the good fight; a mother facing the worst thing a mother can face, yet trusting God; a father who yearns deeply for the healing of his son and a return to family normalcy, and in the midst of the battle, orders his soul to rest in God. Their story is not pleasant or pretty. But it is life, and through their vulnerability, we learn how to struggle, fight, hope, and let go. Without fanfare or pomp, the Gilberts model how Christians ought to walk with God through the valleys of life.

After reading *Journey To The Dance*, I predict you will thank God for every precious moment you have with family members, especially your children. You will reaffirm your belief that regardless of the trial, God is with you….Above all you will want your time on this earth to matter. You will examine your days through the silhouette of David Gilbert's example, and you will resolve to not waste another moment of this precious gift called life."

- **Rick Rigsby**, Ph.D., minister and motivational speaker, former senior lecturer, Department of Communication and Aggie Football Life Skills Coach, Texas A&M University

"*Journey to the Dance* gives detailed and honest insight into not only the medical side of David's fight with cancer, but also the emotional battle that is paramount to everyday survival. Cancer may embody itself in one person, but the battle includes the whole family. Laura Gilbert writes with piercing truth of how cancer ravaged their son and their lives but how God's tenderness carried them through to their final good-bye to their precious David. This is not just a story…it is a real testimony of God's merciful love to strengthen and uphold all of us in desperate times. I laughed, and I cried walking alongside Laura as she skillfully relates her story of caring for her son. *Journey to the Dance* will give everyone a better understanding of how to support and love others during a crisis."

- **Shirley Cothran Barret**, Ph.D., former Miss America, author and public speaker

"Laura Gilbert takes the reader on a very personal journey that we all hope to avoid. Having made that journey myself and now on the other side, I celebrate with Laura. Read this well written story then dance."

- **Ron Hall**, New York Times bestselling author, *Same Kind Of Different As Me* and *What Difference Do It Make*

"This memoir of the journey of faith that the Gilbert family has been through will give each reader an insight to God's grace, strength, and amazing provision through a time of tragedy. Each reader will be captured from the first words of Laura Gilbert as she expresses her heart in only a way that a mother can. My own life, along with that of thousands of students at Texas A&M University and beyond, have been impacted by the legacy of David Gilbert. In fact, each year, one of the most prestigious events held on our campus is the Gilbert Leadership Conference. After reading this memoir, you will think that the words that the Apostle Paul wrote, "I thank God upon each remembrance of you", were specifically penned for the life of David Gilbert."

- **Ben D. Welch, Ph.D.**, professor, Texas A&M University

"Journey To The Dance is a story poured straight from the big, caring hearts of Tom and Laura Gilbert. Their journey through the death of their son David is a testimony to God's amazing grace and promise for a future and a hope."

- **Dr. Joe White**, President Kanakuk Kamps, author and public speaker, founder of "Kids Across America"

"Journey To The Dance is a painfully honest gift as it gives no false hope of overcoming grief quickly or magically. In fact the entire book weaves the details of a real life story. Laura Gilbert reveals the pain and peace, loss and joy coexisting in a broken world. One sees that prayer is real and that it is not always easy in the moment to see the answers to our desperate cries to God."

- **Neil Tomba**, Senior Pastor, Northwest Bible Church, Dallas

"As I read *Journey To The Dance,* I was captivated and deeply touched by the family's continued faith as they raced against the clock to save their son David. The Gilbert's ability to release their son back to God is inspiring and provides the reader with a deep sense of hope despite the circumstances. Laura Gilbert helps the reader truly understand what it is to praise Him in a storm."

- **Karen James**, author, inspirational speaker, widow of Mt. Hood climber Kelly James

"I had the privilege to work with David through his involvement in Student Government at Texas A&M University. His life and faith, as well as that of his family, touched and inspired thousands. Through this book, thousands more will be touched and inspired as well. It is a very open and honest record of their journey together. It is an inspiration to all who have made or will make the same type of journey in their lives. Thank you, Tom and Laura, for sharing it with all of us."

- **Bobby Tucker**, Associate Pastor, Antioch Baptist Church, Conway, Arkansas

JOURNEY TO THE *Dance*

LAURA GILBERT

This book is dedicated to friends we've met along our journey
and parents everywhere who have been shattered by the loss
of a child...we grieve with you.

ACKNOWLEDGMENTS

With love and gratitude I thank my husband, Tom, for his support as I traversed this path of writing. If not for his encouragement, it would have been impossible emotionally. As he also wrote his "Reflections" in the memoir, I'm grateful for the transparency of his heart as he shared the journey alongside of me. I'm thankful for my son, Jonathan, his wife, Stephanie, and my youngest son, Andrew. My family is truly the light of my life.

I acknowledge my wonderful editor, Jan Winebrenner, for her role in this project. I appreciate her wisdom, faithfulness, and encouragement offered when I needed it most, as she tirelessly persevered with me.

For those who fueled my passion to write and held me accountable along the way, thank you: Lisa Stopfel, Gayla Thompson, Cliff Dugosh, Cathy Murray, and Mallory Bida. I will always be grateful to you. It is no coincidence that you were in my life at this time.

For our friends and family, as well as extended family, who became our gracious warriors in battle with us--we will never forget all you have done for our family. Linda and Rick Strickland, Brenda and Tyler Pierson, our "Neighborhood Bible Study", special friends in Dallas and Arlington, Lamar Baptist Church, David's friends-- both college and high school--and their parents, all stood by our side. I thank Carol and Buddy Welter and those who made their way to MD Anderson to bring encouragement and hope, and everyone who prayed for our family. We are deeply indebted, grateful, and forever changed because of what we've experienced.

The Texas A&M leadership conference in David's memory began with Rachel Toppert. From a seed of thought, fourteen Aggies came alongside Rachel and tirelessly worked to form the official conference it is today, the Gilbert Leadership Conference. Our family is grateful for each person who served on the inaugural committee for their perseverance, wisdom and dedication. A very heartfelt thank you to the GLC inaugural committee: Kelly Bjornaas Pettigrew, Peter Boynton, Dillon Dewald, Andrew Greever, Joseph Hildebrand, Paige Holt Langford, Carly Kouba Nance, Jennifer Leftwich Caddou, Joe Licata, Micah Nance, Matthew Pierson, Jay Tom Ratliff, Chris Rogers, Rachel Toppert and Jake West. Our family is blessed by our relationships with each of these, as well as all others who will serve going forward.

To God be the glory. Like David, I felt on many days when I had no strength to walk, I was *carried*. My battle was His and I felt the fullness of His provisions.

.

"What we learn about life through our season of grief propels us to a greater sense of passion for celebrating all that our hearts treasure. We don't wait for a thousand tomorrows. We dance life now and invite those we love to join us."
Susan Duke

CHAPTER 1

The phone rang at 3:10 a.m. Groggy, disoriented, I listened to my son David's voice. "I'm okay, Mom—we're all okay, but a tire blew—the car rolled. We're at the hospital in Sherman. Let me pass the phone to the nurse so she can give you directions here…really, we're okay."

A parent's nightmare played out in my imagination as my husband Tom and I dressed quickly and started the sixty mile drive from our home in Arlington, Texas, to Wilson Jones Hospital near the Texas-Oklahoma border, in Sherman, Texas.

Three teenagers, exhausted from a five-week session as counselors at Kanakuk, a Christian sports camp in Missouri, were alive after the SUV that David was driving rolled three times. Just cuts and bruises, David said. Tom and I drove in silence, at times shuddering as thoughts of what might have been washed over us.

We found the kids unhurt but shaken and stunned. They had taken so many precautions. David's passengers, two girls, were special friends who had ridden with him to help keep him awake and alert for the eight hour drive home from Missouri. David's car had been the lead with two more Kanakuk girls following. They had watched in horror as his Explorer, traveling 75 miles per hour, spun out of control and rolled over and over before finally crashing. David and his passengers, Laura and Makenzie, had been able to crawl out of the wreckage. The Kanakuk friends in the car following, as well as a married couple on the highway, were their good Samaritans. They consoled and wrapped blankets around their shoulders as the three

1

huddled in shock and dismay. It must have felt longer than a few minutes as they waited for emergency vehicles to arrive and take them to the hospital.

"I may have hit a pothole," David told Tom and me when we found him in the emergency room. "That's the only thing I can think of. The tires were practically new." He shook his head, still trying to make sense of it. "I never saw it coming."

Relief hung in the air like a tangible entity. I breathed it in and ordered my thoughts: My son was alive and unbroken. *Thank you, God.*

Seconds later, relief turned to terror and disbelief when the ER doctor, Dr. Goodman, pulled Tom and me aside to speak words that would forever change our lives.

"It looks like David has Hodgkins."

Stunned, unable to focus, Tom and I peered closely at what looked like a cloudy mass on an x-ray taken when David first arrived at the emergency room.

"David seemed to have trouble breathing in the ambulance, so the paramedic thought he might have a chest injury. We took two x-rays. You can see what we're looking at here—the mass is next to David's aorta."

I couldn't speak. I could barely breathe. *It's a mistake,* I thought. *It's all a mistake.*

It was Saturday morning, nearly five by now, and we should all have been home, helping David unload the car, bringing his suitcases and junk in from the driveway. We should have been welcoming him with hugs and hurrying him off to take a long morning nap. I should have been puttering in the kitchen, putting together his favorite breakfast, anticipating the fun of a meal together when he woke up. Instead, I stood in a tiny room in a distant hospital, trying to listen, trying to make sense of the unimaginable.

I knew David was sick. Just two days earlier, Tom and I had driven to Kanakuk to see both David and his brother Andrew, our youngest son. I thought David looked awful. He was pale, scrawny for his six-foot-three height, and a nasty cough plagued him.

I thought back, remembering a nagging cough back in May, when he came home after finishing his freshman year at Texas A&M University. I knew he was tired from exams, so before he left for camp he caught up on sleep—lots of sleep—as well as playing

2

basketball with friends. I recalled a slight cough he took with him to Kanakuk. Five weeks later, he looked and sounded terrible.

"I'll be feeling better soon, Mom," he told me when I saw him at camp. "The nurse checked me out and gave me some meds. It's bronchitis. I'll be fine."

If it was up to David, he *would* be fine. He'd be *terrific*. That's how David lived life. He was excited about his little brother Andrew coming back to Kanakuk as a camper again. He loved everything about the camp: the sports activities, the bonds that were forged with the campers and the other staff and counselors, the opportunities for maturing, both in physical and spiritual ways. He was thrilled to be able to share it all with Andrew at K-2, the high school camp.

David insisted on staying until the final day of closing ceremonies. He needed to say good-bye to his campers, as well as the other counselors, then drive the girls home to the Arlington area. He had told them he'd give them a ride home; that was the plan.

David would get home just a few days before our older son Jonathan would return from a six week course of study in Spain. For the first time in months, our entire family would be united. With Jon, 22, David, 19, and Andrew, 16, Tom and I would pack up again and travel to Colorado for a special time together in the cool of the Rocky Mountains. We would have a few days to enjoy each other before Jon and David went back to college at Texas A&M University and Andrew returned to high school. We would soak all the joy we could out of the remaining days of summer.

The plan changed.

"You need to get David to an oncologist immediately," Dr Goodman told us. "Don't wait. Do it this morning."

Five hours later we found ourselves in a small room at Arlington Memorial Hospital with Dr. Barry Firstenberg, an oncologist. Tom and I pieced together the events that brought us to this place and then waited, helpless and silent, while the doctor studied the x-rays and scans we brought with us. I cringed when he pressed his fingers into the sides of David's neck, then probed and prodded his abdomen and chest.

"We'll need to biopsy a node," Dr. Firstenberg said. And then he spoke that most hated and feared word: Cancer.

My breath caught in my throat. Tom's face turned white and he slumped against the wall. Speechless, appalled, I looked at David.

Shock and uncertainty spread across his features. In that moment, I wanted nothing so much as to cover his ears, wrap my arms around him and hold him until we all awoke from this nightmare.

As if in slow motion, Tom and I both moved toward David.

Each of us was trying to process what we had just heard. My thoughts were a jumble of confusion. I kept going back to the emergency room in Sherman, where I first heard the possibility of Hodgkins. Was that cancer? Was it non-Hodgkins, or Hodgkins? What would happen next?

I remember deliberately telling myself that I would not think about the worst-case scenario. Tom and I had to be hopeful and optimistic, so David could be hopeful and optimistic. We had never dealt with difficulties or challenges by expecting the worst, and we weren't going to start now. David would have the scheduled biopsy and we'd put this behind us. That was all my mind could comprehend.

* * *

Tom's Reflections, June 26, 2004

I have just learned that my son might have cancer. I am not prepared for this. Disbelief passes through me. I feel it in my body. I look at David's face and stumble backwards, regaining my balance against the wall. I try to shape questions; Laura asks some of her own. A blur of color and movement catches my attention and I glance at the TV where a golf tournament is being broadcast. We're a foursome—my three sons and I. Cancer…it can't be.

CHAPTER 2

I should have known life with David would be a wild ride. He was conceived at Disney World. In 1983, Tom and I left two-year-old Jon with my sister Linda and her husband Rick and flew to Florida to explore the newly-opened Epcot Center. We should have expected that a life originating in the Magic Kingdom would be lived at full-speed.

And that was David: open-throttle all the way. Imaginative and stubborn from the start, he learned early to hate the word "no" with ferocity.

"No, David, you can't have dessert until you eat the food on your plate." I said it again, firmly, to be sure my two-year-old understood. He looked around at the family members gathered at Tom's parents' dining room table, took a big breath, and then plunged his face into the plateful of food in front of him. For several minutes he just lay there, face down in the gravy and vegetables, and then the tantrum passed as quickly as a Texas summer storm. He lifted his head, a bit embarrassed, I think, but not unbowed.

David was always the last of our sons to respond to discipline. Long after his brother Jonathan had given in, David still resisted, fighting authority and trying to impose his will. Obstinate and creative, he demanded my attention in ways his older brother didn't. He was fearless and accident prone.

A treasured photo in our family album shows Jon and David standing together in our kitchen, their eyes swollen from crying, their heads bandaged. A backyard playtime turned into a mad dash to the emergency room after Jon hollered, "Watch me!", and then bailed backward out of the swing, crashing into the fence. Jon wailed, I rushed to him, and then shrieked at the sight of gushing blood. So much blood from one little kid's head! Later, at the hospital, I was consoling Jon while the doctor stitched his head when I looked up to see a nurse carrying a bleeding David toward me. A sheepish Tom followed close behind.

"He'll need stitches, too," the nurse said.

"I didn't see him—I was filling out the paperwork," Tom said. He missed David's freefall onto the wooden arm of the couch and only looked up when he heard the screams.

"Any chance you've got a 'two for the price of one' sale tonight?" Tom asked the doctor.

When his younger brother Andrew was born, David was three. He seemed to settle down some, become more manageable, less rambunctious, but he never grew comfortable with limits. David was always looking for ways to climb higher, move faster, reach farther. And he never grew comfortable with the word "No."

"Yes" was David's favorite word.

"Yes" to life.

"Yes" to friends and family.

"Yes" to faith.

And, "yes" to wherever the fun was happening.

Say 'no' to this, David, I thought, as I looked at him lying in a bed in the cancer wing on the third floor of Arlington Memorial Hospital. *Say 'no' with all the stubborn tenacity I know you have in you!*

I felt as though I was caught in a nightmare. It was still Saturday. Only a few hours had passed since we stood in the ER with David and his friends. Another hospital, more terrifying words. More fear. More disbelief.

So many things to do, so much to think about: Monday morning, surgery to remove the node from David's neck for biopsy. Jon, still in Madrid, didn't know about David yet—he was in-flight, heading home to Texas. We would have to speak to him as soon as possible.

Meanwhile, swirls of people moved in and out of David's room, gathering around his bed, flowing out into the hallways, laughing, talking. The crowds continued throughout Saturday and into Sunday. David welcomed friends, joking and telling stories, but I worried about his weariness. I tried to control the flow of people, but again, David said no.

"Mom, I feel fine and I'm enjoying seeing everyone."

At one point, the noise level prompted a nurse to send part of the crowd down the hall to a waiting area. It wasn't long before David walked down there to join them. *He should be resting, saving his strength,* I thought. His cough reminded me that the mass was continuing to grow in his chest, close to his aortic valve. *Shouldn't he be in bed?* But David said no.

David drew his energy from people, from relationships. He would not be our David if he crawled into a hospital bed and slept when there was a gathering down the hall.

Reluctantly, I gave up trying to police the crowd and began doing what I've always been good at: I began a list. I noted over a hundred visitors, friends and family members, who came to the cancer wing that weekend to spend time with David. I recorded each one who came, finding a kind of comfort in my list-making routine and in the obvious fact that David was much loved. But when his grandfather, Pappy, entered the room in a wheelchair, pushed by Tom's sister, a vice gripped my heart. Pappy's bewildered, painful look said it all. No grandfather should have to hear the word "cancer" in the same sentence with his grandson's name.

Respite came at odd times, in funny little ways, during that weekend of waiting. On Sunday afternoon, my sister Linda and her husband Rick brought a canister of homemade ice cream to the hospital. We were missing a family reunion that day, on my father's side, the Ramey family (David's middle name), so they brought some of the dessert fare up to us. The nurses looked the other way while the gang in David's room devoured it.

That same afternoon, Cliff, a special friend of David's, came by and held court, delighting everyone with his stories of Texas A&M. Tom and I had heard about Cliff, but we had never met him. That day, we knew he was someone we would never forget. His exuberant humor and genuine kindness that day was a gift that would keep on giving throughout the months to come.

Cliff worked for the university in the Department of Student Affairs. He had developed strong relationships with Aggie students through the years and in the short time he had known David, he became one of David's staunchest allies. He had a huge network of connections to inform the Aggie family, all ages, of David's situation. Within hours, he sent word to thousands of students and alumni, recruiting an army of prayer support and encouragement for David, and for all of us who loved him.

"You'll never be able to imagine what happens when you combine the power of the Holy Spirit with the Aggie spirit!" Cliff said.

Tom and I chuckled.

David's surgery was on schedule at 11:00 a.m., Monday. Many friends including my sister, Linda, gathered with us to wait.

The minutes passed like hours. When the surgeon appeared and motioned to Tom and me, our friend Paul huddled with our group and prayed.

"The pathologist confirmed the cancer," the doctor told us. "We inserted a chemo port into David's chest while he was under the anesthesia. It will take about three days to determine the exact form of Hodgkins."

Tom and I followed the doctor into David's recovery room. Behind us, I could hear the quiet, steady drone of our friends' voices praying. I felt a strange sense of strength come over me. I wanted to be strong. I had to be strong.

Please make me strong for David, I prayed. But when I saw him, all I could think was, *it's not fair.*

"He has cancer." The words were still ringing in my ears.

Tom and I stood quietly over David, watching him sleep. He woke up with a smile. His first coherent words made me laugh. Lighthearted, funny, he wanted to put *us* at ease. He wanted to relieve *our* pain. I remember the smile, and the awe I felt for my son, but later that day, when I tried to recall what he said, my mind was blank. Tom couldn't recall, either. I vowed that day to keep a journal. I vowed never again to lose the conversations we had with David. I would record his faith, his humor, his fight for life. It was a fight I was determined we would win.

Until David's cancer, I don't think I ever realized how much I hate waiting, how much comfort I derive from action and accomplishment. I like lists, simply for the joy of scratching off items and calling them "done." But cancer doesn't play by my rules, not by anyone's rules, I've learned. Cancer doesn't honor "to-do" lists; it doesn't cooperate with time lines.

8

Cancer makes you wait.

Three days, the doctor had said. Three days until we would have a specific diagnosis. Three days of hoping, praying, fearing, wanting to trust.

Once again, we needed our faithful army to pray for strength and patience for us, for David. Mostly, we needed them to pray that the diagnosis would be Hodgkins Lymphoma, and *not* non-Hodgkins Lymphoma.

Hodgkins Lymphoma has the highest cure rate.

Please, Lord, if it has to be cancer, let it be Hodgkins.

I was comforted to know that many people were praying that same prayer with Tom and me. Several of David's friends were studying abroad and others were on mission trips. The news of his illness spread quickly. All around the world, people who knew David, as well as others who didn't, were talking to God about our son. Already stories about his humor and faith were traveling on Facebook, through email, and phone calls.

David was light-headed and weak after the surgery, so he was not released until the next morning. Again, I chafed at having to wait. I wanted my son home. I wanted to care for him and fuss over him, but at the same time, I felt my inadequacies as a mom in ways I never had before. As a mother of three boys, I had often felt overwhelmed and uncertain, but nothing in my experience had ever left me feeling so helpless. It was just one more thing cancer was teaching me: Cancer can make you feel helpless and afraid.

Once again, I found some comfort in the distraction of my "to-do" list: most items focused on David, but his brothers' needs had to be on there too. We had to figure out how to get Jon home after his cross-Atlantic flight from Madrid. Neither Tom nor I could leave David and drive to Houston to meet him, but we felt strongly that he should hear the details of his brother's illness from a family member.

My brother-in-law Rick offered to drive down to meet Jon. He would drive him to a quiet place where Tom could phone him and share more news. Meanwhile, I would get David settled in his room at home and wait until I could have all my sons with me. I would resist the urge to hold them all tightly and cry over them. I would check my notebook and figure out the next right thing to do.

It wasn't on my list to break down when I watched Jon greet David upon arriving home. The confusion on his face nearly brought

9

me to my knees. Jon tried to hug David gingerly, being careful of his incision and the port inside his chest, but David winced, and then grinned. "Don't worry," he said. "I know I can beat this. I'll be back at A&M before you know it."

Thursday afternoon, July 1st, 2:00 PM, the phone rang. It was Judy, Dr. Firstenberg's nurse, telling us that the official biopsy report was in. David and I would drive to the cancer center where we would meet up with Tom to hear the news from the doctor.

After the initial greetings were out of the way, Dr. F. forged ahead with the details of the pathologist's report. He discussed scans and diagrams; he checked David, pushing and prodding again—his chest, abdomen, arms and neck. He didn't waste any time; the news was grim.

"T-cell Lymphoma," he said. "Acts like leukemia—aggressive and fast-growing. Chemotherapy is the only recourse…a very serious situation."

I could not believe what I was hearing. *This cannot be happening to David!*

David is an athlete. He has youth on his side…this cannot be growing in HIS body.

I wanted to scream, to cry. I wanted to be weak and sink to the floor and sob. I wanted desperately to react to what I was hearing, but David was in the room. Looking at his face, I read his fear and the questions he wanted to ask. I couldn't let my fear add to his. My chest ached with the agony of a broken heart. Even as the pain registered, I felt a surge of strength enter me. I had always known I would fight for my children, but now that the time had come, I felt like a lioness. I might be trembling, but I would not run away and hide in fear. I would do whatever it took to help David, to get him through this. I believed God could hear our prayers.

And I knew my David. He was the most stubborn child on the planet. If anyone could beat this, he could.

It was time to focus.

I pulled out my spiral notebook for medical notes and began writing.

A deluge of decisions had to be made.

Dave's cough reminded me of the dire circumstances before us.

* * *

Tom's Reflections, June 30, 2004

We should be in Colorado right now. We should be golfing, hiking, white-water rafting. But we're not. I'm sitting at my computer, spending every spare minute researching types of cancer on the internet. We are all struggling to understand what is going on with David. His cancer is very aggressive, fast growing. It is the most dangerous form for a young man to have. We have to move quickly—it is growing so fast we don't have time for a second opinion until after we get started on the first round of treatments. I feel the need for full reliance on the doctors.

I'm learning that you can never be prepared for an event such as this. It feels like my family is in total disarray. I am lonely and uncertain. I'm trying to make sense of how a loving God can allow something like this to happen. It seems to be a total disconnect.

I am feeling helpless as a father.

Yet, as a believer in a sovereign God, His provision occurs at those moments you cannot think straight. The Holy Spirit has guided us and prompted us. It is still a time of great uncertainty: my middle son has an aggressive form of cancer. At the same time, I am so proud of my family. We discussed our opportunity to truly rely on God through our battle. We began praying that we would all walk in harmony with God's intentions. David, surrounded by the unknowns and uncertainties of cancer, allowed himself to be filled with God's comfort and peace. What a time for a father to observe each of his sons' faithfulness and love for our God.

CHAPTER 3

We had no time to waste. David needed chemotherapy immediately, but the Fourth of July holiday would cost us valuable time. Treatment couldn't begin until the sixth—six days of delay for the treatment needed to save his life. Once again we found ourselves waiting. As incredible as that seemed to me, for David it was like a gift. He would have time to get himself ready for the battle that lay ahead. For David, that meant time with his close friends and family.

Our home began to look like a transit station. People came and went, like masses through a revolving door, delivering food and beverages of all kinds. Some lingered only long enough to talk a bit, attempt lighthearted conversation; others stayed, wishing for something more they could do for us. The doorbell and phone rang constantly. David loved it. His cell phone, tossed out of his rolling Explorer, had survived the crash, and one of his friends found it on the ground beside the mangled SUV and brought it to him. David lost no time in making and getting calls. His phone never stopped ringing.

To the unknowing, our household looked like a party site. But the laughter belied the shock and disbelief that each visitor brought through the door. Fear hovered near the threshold.

"We can't have this," Tom whispered to me as we opened the door to yet another stunned, tearful visitor. Together, we agreed: we refused to be morose. We would not tolerate sadness or despair—not in ourselves, and not in anyone coming into our home. We would keep things upbeat and positive. It would take all our energy, but for

David's sake, and for our own, we would not give in to the fear that shadowed our smiles of welcome each time the doorbell rang.

Among the visitors, our closest friends and relatives hovered close, their familiar faces more comfort than I could express. My sister Linda, with her husband Rick, with their kids (friends as well as cousins) were in and out constantly, watching for the next thing they could do to help or encourage us. Our dearest friends, Brenda and Tyler, never let us out of their sight. Their daughter Megan, one of David's best friends, was ever-present. Tom's sister and brother-in-law, Stacey and Bill, came as often as possible.

It didn't take long for a kind of "division of labor" to evolve. Linda and Brenda took charge of communications, brainstorming how they would man the phones, answer the innumerable emails already accumulating, and coordinate the delivery of meals that scores of people continued to offer, in addition to the ones that just showed up at the door in the hands of caring visitors.

I was overwhelmed. Overwhelmed by the generosity of friends, both ours and David's; overwhelmed by the level of activity circling around me; overwhelmed at the immensity of what lay ahead for me, for David, for all of our family.

Some time that week, my friend Karen arrived and handed me a leather journal. "Write about this journey," she said. "You'll enjoy reading it later." I had started writing, and now I had a nice leather journal. Karen, my dear friend from church, was a godsend. She was that friend that always did the right thing at the right time.

At times, the hours passed in a blur. People swirled around me, coming and going, almost dreamlike, but I was always acutely aware of the constant presence of Andrew and Jon. Others came and went—others, well-loved and appreciated, but for Tom and me, our sons were our strongest support. Rallying around David, and staying close, Jon and Andrew were an ever-present source of strength for us. Jon cancelled his plans to work as a counselor at Kanakuk's second session so he could participate in David's chemo treatments. He studied Andrew's golf tournament schedule and arranged to drive his brother to his out-of-town tournaments.

Our sons who had been such a source of joy and chaos since birth now stood with us as extraordinary young men of purpose and courage, all three of them. Jon, David, and Andrew: each of them committed to each other, to our family; each of them willing to learn new lessons about walking with the God they had trusted since childhood.

In my sweetest dreams of motherhood, I had never imagined that children could infuse a life with such deep pain and such exquisite joy. My own children were doing just that in ways that defy description. When I found myself weeping, at times I was at a loss to know which emotion was stronger: joy, or grief.

As far back as I can remember, I always wanted to be a wife and mother. I married Tom soon after I graduated from Baylor in 1978. I taught elementary school for a while, but as soon as Jonathan was born, I decided to stay home with him. I didn't want to miss even a single moment of his childhood. When David arrived, we chose his name with great thought, praying that he and his brother would share a loving relationship, like the David and Jonathan in the Bible. When Andrew came along, three years later, our family felt complete. I was outnumbered, yes, but the men in my life were more precious to me than words could express.

We loved summer breaks and couldn't wait to plan vacations. If money was scarce, we did "stay-cations", visiting Dealy Plaza, local museums, water parks and baseball games. Tom took off work like it was a real vacation. When Nolan Ryan pitched his no hitter, Jon and one of his friends were with Tom at Ranger Stadium.

When we could afford it, we took the boys camping, took them snow skiing in New Mexico and Colorado. We loved tubing in Texas' hill country and rafting the Brown River in Colorado. The boys planned occasional father-son trips that left me at home, but I was delighted that they were building strong relationships, so I didn't complain. Once, while playing in a golf tournament, Jon won a "closest to the hole" contest. The prize was two tickets to the Super Bowl game in San Diego; he took his brother David. The friendship and trust that began forming in early childhood among all three of our sons was now, for us all, a source of strength none of us had ever imagined needing.

One evening, during those days of waiting, we sat down to dinner together—a quiet dinner, no visitors, no phone calls, just the five of us. We had devoured much of the food our friends had brought, and the desserts were running low. Only one slice of cake was left. Andrew reached for it.

"If the cancer man thinks he gets that last slice, he can forget it! It's mine!" Andrew said, diving in for the last slice.

Shocked, I looked at David and held my breath. His sudden loud guffaw instantly sent us all into peals of laughter.

I prayed a prayer of thanksgiving: for my sons, for their sense of humor, and for the healing power of laughter. I determined to listen at all times for any hint of humor I could enjoy. I resolved to indulge in any small serving of laughter with all the passion of a glutton at a pie-eating contest.

I had no idea of how often, and how severely, that resolve would be tested.

Each day of waiting brought reminders of the urgency of David's situation. The mass was growing. His breathing was becoming more labored. I could see that he was preparing himself mentally, emotionally, and spiritually for the fight of his life. He joined Tom and me in researching the specific diagnosis we had learned from the oncologist: T-cell Lymphoblastic Leukemia/Lymphoma. It was lymphoma that acted like leukemia, a kind of lymphoma that attacks only about 5% of all lymphoma patients.

We learned that this type of cancer most typically attacks adolescent males between the ages of 18-25. Our hopes that David's youth would be in his favor as he fought this disease were destroyed. We were dismayed to learn that his age was against him. The hormone levels of young men his age drive the disease at a frighteningly fast speed, making it hard to keep pace with its deadly track.

Get a second opinion: that's the conventional wisdom in a medical crisis. But there was nothing conventional about David's condition. The fast-growing mass that reached for a strangle-hold on his aorta did not give us the luxury of more time. It wasn't going to pause to wait for Tom and me to deliberate over a list of other doctors who would not be able to fit David into their schedule for weeks, but it was agony to think about our limited options. We had to go forward. David's disease was advancing. We couldn't afford to let it get any further ahead of us. The decision to begin chemo wasn't negotiable. It would begin, as planned, based on Dr. Firstenburg's diagnosis and recommendation. Thankfully, our friends in the medical field confirmed our opinion that the Arlington Cancer Center, as well as Dr. F, held strong reputations.

Just get started! That was our mantra.

David had already begun to bond with his doctor. He liked the idea that Dr. Firstenburg gave him his cell phone number. He gave David permission to call him anytime, day or night.

It was a simple gesture, but David felt respected and encouraged.

"If just one person comes to know Jesus because of this experience, it will be worth it," he told his cousin, Laura. "I'm trusting God," he said.

And he meant it.

The night before his chemo treatments were to begin, well loved friends and men from our church began arriving to pray over David. With one purpose, they gathered in our family room and hovered around him. I listened in as Tom, Jon and Andrew joined this group of men seeking God's healing power in and through David.

After the last "amen", David stepped up to each man and thanked him for his prayers and encouragement. His tall frame enveloped each of them when he hugged them and said the words Tom and I were too moved to speak: "This meant so much to me and my family...you mean so much to us."

The gesture of companionship and the time of prayer seemed to buoy us all. David was prepared, as prepared as he could be.

* * *

Tom's Reflections, July 5th, 2004

We are a sports-minded family. The guys played all the sports when they were young and eventually grew to love basketball and golf. Why does a father want his sons to participate in sports? They learn teamwork, commitment, honor, and a desire to compete and win. I have loved teaching my sons, sharing their experiences. Like my boys, I have failed tests, lost games, broken up with girlfriends, gotten in all kinds of trouble—but this—this challenge I have never faced. I cannot tell David that I know what he's going through. I can't say, "I've been there, son. It will be all right."

Tonight, David and I watched "The Last Samurai" together. We watched the warriors prepare themselves for their last big battle near the end of the movie. I can't help but think of the similarities:

his chemo begins tomorrow. He will begin treatment to stop a powerful and dangerous cancer growing in his body. He is preparing for a great battle. He is preparing with his almighty God. He is putting on the whole armor of God.

I know I am watching a miracle as my family moves forward together in a powerful way—all of us—to fight with David. As David prepares himself, we prepare ourselves too. We each have roles that we need to play. Even so, I am going to bed with thoughts of apprehension and concern. We simply don't know what the future holds.

I worry that my prayers are inadequate.

How I wish it were me, and not David.

CHAPTER 4

"The best chance to fight lymphoma cancer is the first chance. We don't want to have to do this again."

Tom and I reminded each other of Dr. Firstenberg's words as we mulled over the notes I had written down in his office.

We wanted to be as prepared as possible.

We reviewed the protocol he had laid out for David.

The first effort would be aimed at shrinking the mass that was now softball-sized and pressing against his air tube and aorta. Second, David would undergo periodic spinal fluid tests to be sure the cancer hadn't spread to the central nervous system. Third, David's stem cells would be harvested in the event that a stem cell transplant would be needed in the future. Fourth, his chest and mid-sternum area would be radiated as the last measure to ensure there would be no reoccurrence of the cancer.

Three rounds of various chemo drugs would complete a cycle, Dr. F. had told us. In between rounds, David would be given medication to counteract the side effects of the chemo and to help his blood counts recover before being blasted again with the next chemo round.

This was our first chance, our best chance, for David. On paper it looked daunting, but we were ready.

An eerie combination of disbelief and determination accompanied Tom and me as we walked into the Infusion Place at Arlington Cancer Center with David.

The head oncology nurse, Eileen, met us, prepared for David's arrival with a folder full of detailed orders from Dr. F. She smiled, chatted with David, and led us to the infusion area. In the middle of this large room stood the nurses' station. Along the perimeter of the room were many small areas, each set with four recliners with TVs attached to each one. There was space for not just the cancer patient, but for family members as well. Already the room was filling with patients scheduled for chemo treatments. David was not alone.

As Eileen began to get David comfortable in a recliner, she discussed with him everything that was soon to be pumped into his body. (He had already been told to wear a button down shirt and not a t-shirt since the tubes were connected through the port in his chest.) She wanted him to know *everything* and David *wanted* to know. Tom and I looked at one another and he nodded to me to write down all of our questions. I started our list. So much information was coming at us.

This first day of treatment, David would receive an infusion of a conglomerate of fluids to prepare his body for the chemo that would come later in the day. For six hours he would be infused, just to get ready for what came next. Already, I felt overwhelmed. I was thankful for the calm and friendly manner of Eileen and the other nurses.

As soon as David was hooked up, he smiled, said, "Here we go," and winked.

I wanted to burst into tears, but I made myself smile back at him.

Sitting there together, in that small space, dominated by the recliner and IV paraphernalia, we made an effort at small talk. David joked, trying to put Tom and me at ease. In a few moments, he closed his eyes and grew quiet, listening to music on his small CD player.

Occasionally, Tom or I roused him to ask how he was feeling, if he was feeling anything different.

"Nothing yet," David answered. "It just feels weird being hooked up and having this stuff going into my chest."

Shortly before noon, we started talking about lunch. Eileen said David could eat anything he was hungry for. Soon David was wolfing down a chicken sandwich and a milk shake. Little did I know in a few days we would be begging him to try, *just try*, and eat a little something, *anything*.

After David had eaten, Tom and I felt comfortable leaving him for a little while. We drove to our church and went to the prayer room. Cindy, a friend who happened to be there, told us that many people were fasting and praying for David on this, his first day of treatment. We were deeply touched at the thought of so many caring enough, committed enough, to fast for David—David, who had just gobbled his favorite fast food meal from Chick-fil-A®. It was nice to have something to chuckle about.

We returned to find David slowly moving back to his area from the bathroom, pulling his IV pole with the almost empty-pouches along with him. I hated seeing him move with such effort, but the massive volume of fluids being infused into his body made him have to get up and down many times that day, each time with increasing difficulty.

Eileen came often to check on David. Each time, she reassured, encouraged; each time, it seemed, she had more information for us. I tried to make sense of the detailed instructions we would take home with us.

Eileen explained that, while the chemo was attacking the cancer cells, it was also killing good cells, which is why there are so many side effects—too many to count. And we had to be prepared for them. When we took David home, I would have to administer the meds on a timely basis. I felt my anxiety build.

We would have to stay ahead of the nausea, Eileen told us. We couldn't allow it to get ahead of David, and *everything* had the *potential* for nausea.

We will stay ahead of it, David, I vowed silently. *I won't let you suffer more than you have to.*

"We'll get through this together," Eileen reassured me. "You'll do just fine"

Her confidence gave me confidence.

Before we left the Infusion Place, Eileen brought David a package that looked like a small canvas carry-on bag.

"This is your computer, and this is the timer that works with it," Eileen told us, pointing out the parts of what looked to me like a complicated piece of equipment. "The computer and timer will keep the infusion going after you leave us today, David. From 4:30 this afternoon until 7:30 tonight, and then again from 4:30 to 7:30 in the morning, the computer will release Cytoxin, the chemo drug, and

Mesna, the fluid that will protect your bladder from the effects of the Cytoxin." She pointed to two pouches connected to the computer pack.

Tom and I listened intently, trying to understand all the instructions. I wrote as fast as I could, trying not to scribble, knowing mistakes were not an option for us, for David. At the same time, my mind was flooded with thoughts of "What if?"

What if the timer failed?

What if the computer crashed?

Eileen's final instructions: "Drink plenty of liquids and urinate often. Call me if you have any burning sensation when you go to the bathroom."

Weak and depleted, David mustered a smile and answered, "I will. See you all tomorrow, same time, same place."

He moved slowly down the hall, flanked by Tom and me, connected to a pump on a rolling pull-cart that would go everywhere he went for the next 24 hours.

* * *

Tom's Reflections, July 6, 2004

David is pulling a canvas bag on wheels with him as he moves around the house. It holds a computer and the chemo chemicals. The computer controls the release of the chemo which flows directly into his body through the port placed in his chest. I don't trust the computer. After David goes to bed, I slide into his room at 11:00 p.m. to see if the computer is working. It is. I get up again around 3:00 a.m. and check again. Yes- the computer is working. Can you believe this? As David sleeps this first night, he has chemo roaring through his body, trying to reduce the size of the mass in his upper chest. I can feel the strain on my mind and body. I can only fathom the strain on David's mind and body. This should not happen to anyone.

CHAPTER 5

Watching David grimace and stifle a moan, I cringed. He was lying face-down, his head lower than his feet, enduring the painful procedure of withdrawing spinal fluid to be tested for the presence of cancer cells. It was day two of his treatment. He was trying to be brave, but each time the doctor inserted needles into his spine, Tom and I clutched each others' hands and held our breath, praying that the cancer had not spread to his spine or his central nervous system. When the results came back negative, our relief was palpable.

The good news encouraged us as we walked next door to the Infusion Place. Once again, David took his seat in a recliner and let the nurses hook him up to the IV. This time, he received an infusion of the anti-nausea drug, Zofran. Two hours later, we left again, heading home with the backpack computer and timer and pouches of Cytoxin and Mesna. As soon as we arrived, David headed for the dining room table. It was covered with a thousand puzzle pieces.

David loved puzzles. He could sit for hours searching for the right pieces, fitting them together until the picture made sense.

There he sat, moving the pieces around, answering his cell phone when it rang, and chatting softly. He was tired, I could tell. He seemed listless. I wondered if he was thinking about the puzzle that his life had become.

Hours passed. David said little to Tom and me.

I prayed, mostly.

Please, Lord, let the Cytoxin work.

The next day we returned to the Infusion Place.

And the next.

Only an order for blood work changed our routine. On those days, we drove to the Cancer Center.

Every day, the Infusion Place or the Cancer Center, some days, both.

My car could have navigated on auto-pilot, never varying from the route, not even to avoid a pothole.

"You hit it again, Mom. It's there—right there, every day! Every single morning, Mom! Don't you see it?"

A pothole on the entrance ramp to I-30 was, to me, a negligible concern; for David, that day, feeling sick and weary, it was an opportunity for a small gesture of frustration amid the huge and daunting drama that his life had become.

David, who endured chemo and needles and nausea without a murmur, found a safe a venue for his irritation: Mom's driving.

I was surprised—I'd hardly noticed the pothole. And then I felt a strange mixture of sadness tinged with thankfulness: this was David, being a kid, if only for a moment. What teenager, forced to be a passenger in a parent's car, doesn't have something to say about the driving?

A hint of normalcy enveloped us in the car that morning, and I welcomed it.

I wasn't surprised that David so quickly became friends with many at the Infusion Place. Each time we arrived, he chatted with the staff at the front desk. Making his way to his recliner, he greeted everyone he passed. And each time we went, I thought, *they are all so much older than David. This is just so wrong.*

Tom and I got used to seeing the chemo patients interact with one another, stopping to chat, never leaving without a smile, a touch, a word of encouragement, like traveling companions who had logged many miles together. Each one stopped by David's chair as if he were the newest adoptee in a large, eclectic family; as if they'd known him forever and loved him already. Each one spoke, some joked, some touched his shoulder before saying good-bye until the next treatment date.

Their hearts ached for David—it was etched in their faces. Their eyes carried the unspoken message: *This shouldn't be happening to you.*

Seeing their tenderness, their kindness, I thought, *I wish it weren't happening to you, too, David. And I wish it weren't happening to them.*

But cancer isn't selective. Cancer is many things, but not that. Capricious, but not guileless, it attacks when and where it will.

David's conversations with other patients at the Infusion Place helped him recognize what was happening in his body.

"Your taste buds are changing," someone told him one day. "You aren't going to like some of the foods you used to love."

It was true. David's appetite was changing.

Our friends were still bringing us food—David's old favorites—but he wasn't interested in eating. Even when they were willing to cook *anything* to tempt him, David just couldn't stomach the idea of food. Brenda's containers of macaroni and cheese began showing up, along with meat and veggies and wonderful cobblers—foods David used to love. But at mealtimes, he simply picked at the dishes, moving the food around, sometimes laying his head down on the table, and finally getting up to move away from the sights and smells.

As his weight continued to drop, his hair began to fall out. Large patches dropped from his scalp, leaving him with the gaunt and haunted look of a cancer patient. I caught myself searching his face often, desperately hoping to see there the vibrancy of his grin, the irrepressible spark that could enliven a room. But he was too sick to offer more than a feeble smile.

Back pain began to trouble him right away after the first spinal test. We learned that a nerve had been slightly damaged, but the resulting pain wasn't slight; he couldn't stand up straight. I spoke to Dr. F's nurse, Judy, about this and we soon had a prescription for pain pills. Since David had never been a complainer, Tom and I knew that he had to be close to agony to ask for one.

By Friday of the first week of treatment, the doctor ordered changes in David's chemo drugs. My instructions for his home care had to be adjusted. Once again I felt the inadequacy of a mother watching her child suffer. I spent a lot of time with David's nurses, Derek and Mary, who had become his daily companions at the Infusion Place. They were getting to know David well, and they had answers for the many questions I had for them. They knew how David's body was going to react to the killer chemicals he was taking. They had detailed instructions for how I was to administer the new meds at home, and they offered suggestions for David that would help him cope with the changes in his body: such simple things, like brush your teeth gently so your gums don't bleed and so you don't develop a mouth sore; eat small amounts of food often during the day.

Caring for David, at times, felt like trial and error. It was obvious his nausea medication wasn't working, and all we could do was try another one. If the next one didn't work, and it often didn't, we had to try yet another one. It was several tries before we found relief for him.

Round two of David's chemo protocol required Vincristine and the drug Adriamycin, nick-named The Red Devil. David's new friends at The Infusion Place warned him about it—the appearance of the bag of red fluids struck dread in the hearts of the most seasoned cancer patients. His companions sent him sympathetic nods when the nurse arrived carrying the red bag for David's IV pole. It wasn't long before he understood: his anti-nausea meds were able to prevent him from vomiting, but nothing could completely wipe out the awful waves of nausea that overcame him.

One night, during those miserable days, the doorbell rang just as we were finishing dinner. Once again I had watched David pick at his food, silently praying he would be able to tolerate just a little more, *please, just another bite.* Everyday his clothes hung more loosely on his frame. Everyday another handful of hair fell out. Everyday his energy level fell more sharply. The sudden ringing of the doorbell diverted me from what was becoming a typical mealtime monologue in my head, full of questions and fearful dread.

Tom answered the door and I heard a loud shout from the porch.

"It's Shave for Dave Day!"

Three of David's buddies from A&M burst into the house, with a girlfriend in tow, carrying clippers, shears, and a camera. Amid great hilarity and joking, the three guys took turns sitting for the shave while the rest of us snapped pictures, before and after.

"Wherever David's Aggie friends are, heads are being shaved today!" the kids told us.

That hot summer evening, scores of guys—Aggies, all of them—scattered in various places, were going bald and beautiful in support of David.

Tom and I were in awe. David was in heaven!

Laughing, enjoying the moment, for all of us it was a bright spot in an otherwise dark place.

On July 16th, David's 20th birthday, he came home from a chemo treatment to find his bedroom decorated with crepe paper. His friends Mallory and Louise had come over to make sure he knew his friends were thinking about him and celebrating his birthday. They left a stuffed monkey on his desk holding balloons and a card. Our dear friend Tyler wrote a poem for David, and he and Megan delivered it that same evening. It read:

A Host of Caddies for Davo

I can't help but think what God has done
Surrounding me with caddies.
Though some may call them angels
They're friends, moms, and daddies.

I will not face this fight alone.
They all will pray for me.
And Satan, the very best you have
Is double and triple bogey.

There may be days that I am down
But never will be lame.
I'm leaning on the Everlasting One
And friend, we got Game.

I have faced a two iron, straight uphill
Against the wind, no doubt.
But I set my sights, determined,
And for birdie putted out.

Though traps and rough will line my path,
These hazards are only for a while
I've got Jesus and His caddies,
And that will help me smile.

When Sunday afternoon rolls around

The only scene you'll see
Is me surrounded by a host of caddies
As Jesus seals the Victory!

David was battling nausea, as he always did after a chemo infusion, but he was delighted by the gifts and the sweet message of the poem. For all of us, his friends' simple gestures gave us some much needed laughter and opened our hearts to welcome hope, something we could never get enough of.

Hope swelled to a celebration a few days later when a chest x-ray showed that the mass in David's chest had shrunk.

"The Cytoxin worked," Dr. Firstenberg told us as he studied the film.

Tom and I looked at each other, then at David. A huge grin spread over his face. We were all speechless with joy.

For days I had been telling myself that the treatment outcome had to be good—*it just had to be.* Hadn't David's cough been subsiding? Wasn't that a good indication that the treatment was working? No one in our family had even considered the possibility of failure. But in that moment, standing there with David and Tom, I was surprised to hear what sounded like relief in the doctor's voice. Had he not been certain?

It was a question I didn't want to explore too deeply. I wanted to luxuriate in the good news. I wanted to let myself feel grateful and hopeful.

We had made progress. *Thank you, Lord.*

We had won on one battle front. Our soldier was standing strong.

I wanted to savor this victory, if only for a moment. In only a few hours, we would have to return to the war zone.

David still had T-cell cancer, in the form of nodes in his neck and arm-pit. The mass in his chest was shrinking, but he was still sick. We still had much fighting ahead for us.

Weekly spinal taps were added to David's treatment regimen. The pain was excruciating, but each test reported that his spinal fluid was clear; the cancer had not spread to his spine. The joy of this news was tempered only by the intensity of David's suffering.

The best times were those brief periods between chemo treatments when David felt slightly better. It was during one of those times that Andrew and Jon burst into the house at dinner time. We heard them shouting in the utility room, golf clubs clanging. Sunburned, and still sweating, they were both grinning widely, hardly containing their excitement.

"Somebody ask Andrew how he played today at Doral Tesoro!" Jon said.

David was the first to ask. "Did you place, Andrew?"

"I didn't just place, I came in first!" He tried to act smug.

"Congratulations, bro! You're taking after me," David said, laughing. "What did you shoot? Who came in second? How many birdies did you have? Let me see your score card!"

The barrage of questions continued, with Andrew and David comparing their best scores and congratulating each other on being such amazing golfers.

"Hey, I had a little to do with this," Jon said. "Not only did I drive him to the tournament, I gave him golf tips all the way there! Coaching by Jon, no charge!"

"Okay, so who else in this family has won a golf tournament?" David kept the banter going.

It was just like the old days, the days before cancer—the days when the boys were carefree and fun-loving. Jon and David loved to grill their little brother and critique his game and give him tips. And Andrew reveled in their attention.

It was a moment to relish. The next night we were back to our familiar routine.

We spent hours every evening going over each day's events. We discussed David's treatments, went over any doctor's comments, and reviewed how far we had come, how far we still had to go. We were still intent on getting a second opinion, or even a third. We hadn't given up on that, even though David's chemo treatments were in full swing. It was my job to gather all the pertinent scans and reports to forward to a lymphoma specialist in Dallas. David's biopsy slides would be sent to UT Southwestern Medical- Pathology Department for a second read.

Always, it seemed as though there was so much to do, and when it was done, even more was waiting to be done. We would have fallen under such a heavy load if friends hadn't come alongside us to help us carry the load.

"God-winks," one friend liked to say: those rays of sunshine that God sends us when the darkness gets too oppressive. If not for the glimpses of light, the darkness would have been too much. Both David's friends and ours appeared at the exact moments when we needed what only they could bring. At times, I struggled to make sense of the intense and opposing feelings in my heart: the awful grief of watching David suffer, right there alongside the sweet joy of being loved and ministered to by friends.

Meals arrived every other evening now. Friends left cases of bottled water and Gatorade® on our front porch each Monday, along with cards and messages of loving encouragement. Care packages for David arrived in the mail nearly every day. Often we returned home from the cancer center to find that a friend had scrubbed and vacuumed our house and cleaned out our two neglected refrigerators. Friends who knew David brought him 1000-piece puzzles.

Jon and Andrew spent many hours keeping David company during his three-to-four hour transfusions at the Infusion Place. Jon became our "go-to" guy, running to the pharmacy, making quick grocery story runs when Tom and I were caring for David. Jon was Andrew's ride to golf tournaments that Tom and I had to miss. He and Andrew sat with David while he worked puzzles, watched golf tournaments and other sports events with him, and made themselves an integral part of the battle plan for David's life.

Sometime in those early weeks of David's chemo treatments, Jon asked to bring his girlfriend Stephanie to Arlington to stay with our family for a few days. It was a complicated time: David so sick; trips to the cancer treatment dominating our schedule. But it felt right to me. I wanted Stephanie to come.

The first time I met her, I knew Stephanie was one of God's "winks." Having her with us, in our home, for three days, would be a welcome diversion for me; she would bring a fresh wind of humor and life into our home. Plus, I always welcomed the company of another woman in our household outnumbered by men. But I had to admit, I felt a little nervous; I wanted everything to be perfect for her visit.

They were due to arrive at any minute. David and I would make it home from the cancer center and another round of chemo in time to greet them if we hurried.

We pulled into the garage; I helped David into the house. He made it only as far as the kitchen before vomiting into the sink.

I was horrified!

David leaned on me and I helped him into a chair. Rushing back to the kitchen I rinsed the sink and sprayed air freshener. A minute later Jon and Stephanie walked through the door.

In that moment, Stephanie stepped into our family's messy, painful circumstances without a flinch or a grimace, and right into our hearts. For the next three days, she became part of the family cheering squad as we watched every minute of the Olympics broadcast from Athens, Greece.

Our family had always loved sports, but during that period of chemo, for David, watching sports, getting caught up in the competition and the beauty of speed and strength, the diversion was a welcome respite. David really got excited when home town hero Jeremy Wariner competed in the 400 meter race.

"Ten minutes, everyone!" David called out. "Stephanie, get in here! Jeremy races in ten minutes."

Stephanie quickly caught on that this was not just another race.

"I played Little League with Jeremy!" David hollered. "And I played against him in city league basketball! We knew each other!"

"Yeah, and I coached him in baseball," Tom said, as he sat down in front of the TV.

"Wow! I'm impressed," Stephanie said, listening to the men in the family try to take some credit for Jeremy's success.

Even George, the family dog, joined the clamber as we all leaped to our feet to shout and cheer as Jeremy crossed the finish line in first place to win the gold medal.

That night was an oasis for me: seeing my family laughing, cheering, bonding; seeing Stephanie settle in with her sweet, calm manner. Her first visit was too short, but it would be the first of many.

David's third round of chemo protocol—the last in Dr. Firstenberg's treatment plan—called for a change in tactics: a much harsher combination of chemo drugs. Methotrexate and ARA-C would be used to attack the cancer cells. It would be the most destructive toward the healthy cells too. The side effects would be the worst yet.

Dr. Firstenberg offered to put David in the hospital during this cycle of chemo—this was common practice for many patients, especially older patients—but David was young, and he wanted to be at home. I was able to administer the drugs to counter the side effects as well as anyone at the hospital, so David got his wish.

Once the infusion was finished and the killer chemo drugs were at work in his body, it was time for me to get to work. For the next three days, every six hours, I gave him antibiotics and put drops in his eyes, but I couldn't do anything about the chemo's effect on his blood count. In the first couple of days after the infusion of this worst of the chemo drugs, David's blood count dropped dangerously low. Over the next week he needed multiple blood transfusions to boost his platelets. Each transfusion worked for only a day or two before the platelets dropped again. Each time, David's strength took a nose dive. Sometimes he was so weak I had to help him out of the car and into a wheelchair just to get him into the hospital. At this point, his transfusions included drugs to stimulate his bone marrow to produce platelets. I worried constantly about his immune system. Would he be able to fight off an untimely infection? Could his body withstand even the mildest cold or flu bug? Dr. F wanted him to wear a mask one weekend, which he agreed to, except when he was in his bedroom alone.

Like most people, I knew family and friends who had endured cancer. I'd heard the stories of chemo therapy—the nausea, the hair loss. But nothing I ever heard or imagined prepared me to watch my son suffer like this. The misery this latest chemo drug produced was nothing I could have ever expected.

"It feels like I have a mass growing in my throat," David told me. He didn't, of course, but the membranes in his throat and mouth were so dry he could hardly swallow. He didn't even want to try. The nutritional supplements I researched and diligently set before him every day became irrelevant. He could barely tolerate sips of water and wanted nothing to do with food. He became so dehydrated he needed daily infusions of fluids at the Cancer Center.

For ten days, the chemo drug raged in David's body, creating all the misery and agony predicted. On day eleven, he awoke feeling better.

"I'm hungry, Mom," he called from his bedroom.

My son wanted to eat, and I felt like dancing. I flitted around the kitchen, pulling out pans and dishes, all the while thinking this would be the most important meal I had ever cooked. I don't remember what it was, but I'll never forget David's smile while he ate it. He was weak, but hallelujah! He was hungry! The killer chemo drugs had finally vacated his body. It was cause for a celebration.

For a few days, David would feel normal, but we knew it would be *only* a few days. That small window of time between chemo treatments—that luxurious space in his life where he could play and relax—was getting smaller with every subsequent round of chemo. Yet, everyday Tom and I prayed, *Lord, just give him a few days to be a kid again, to have some fun with his friends, to live without pain and nausea, to be normal and enjoy the things normal kids get to do during summer break.*

Just let him be normal.

I ached for David. He refused to complain, except about potholes, but his illness was taking a terrible toll. Had it been only weeks ago that he was active, muscular and energetic? Now, he was too tired for fun and adventure; his thick wavy hair had fallen out and my heart hurt when I saw how skinny he had become. Withdrawal replaced his normally outgoing, fun-loving manner.

Cancer's cruelty weighed heavy on me. I prayed for David, for all of us, to be able to survive this awful disease without learning to hate, without becoming bitter and angry.

Dr. Firstenberg ordered a CT scan for August 13th. It would mark the end of the first cycle of David's cancer treatment. We would learn how effective it had been.

We would learn if we had reason to celebrate, or reason to grieve.

We showed up at the doctor's office, the three of us, Tom and David and I, our thoughts a battleground: hope trying hard to defeat dread.

Please, God...

David headed off for yet another chest x-ray. A few moments later, we gathered again in Dr. Firstenberg's office and heard him say it: "The mass is gone."

My breath stuck in my throat. I couldn't breathe.

"The first cycle of chemo treatment was effective," Dr. Firstenberg said.

I looked at Tom, then at David. We couldn't speak. For a moment we just soaked in the good news.

Throughout the weeks of treatment, within our family, we had refused to even speak aloud of the possibility of failure; we tiptoed carefully around the huge, terrifying elephant in the room—the tension between hope and dread.

"There's always a chance the chemo won't work," Dr. Firstenberg said. "If it hadn't eradicated the tumor, David would have died quickly."

He put into words what we had never let ourselves imagine. Suddenly, the reality of success slammed into my chest. Relief took my breath away.

Thank you, Lord, thank you. I wept joyful tears of relief.

So invested was I in the success of David's treatment that the relief was almost debilitating in its intensity. For days after the good news, I felt as though I was swinging on a pendulum of emotions. At one moment I felt the euphoria of a mother whose son has returned from the grave; at the next, I felt empty, drained.

We all knew that, while David was out of immediate danger, his body still hosted dangerous cancerous t-cells. They made their presence known in the nodes in his neck and his arm pit, but for now, we weren't letting ourselves think about that. We were intent on celebrating. David felt good enough to pick up his life again, calling friends, spending hours on Facebook. He asked me to bake cookies for all the nurses at the Infusion Place. It was a request I gladly granted.

* * *

Tom's Reflections, August 13, 2004

Today there is an unspoken tenseness in Dr. F's office. What will the CT scan look like? The cough is gone, so that has to mean the chemo is working, doesn't it? The mass must be smaller. Where is Dr. F? What is taking so long? Is that a bad sign? My mind is racing. Negative thoughts dominate. I glance outside: cars pass on the street, people laugh and talk. Life continues to move on as if all were normal, as if all were well with the world.

Dr. F comes in. The news is good. The news is <u>great!</u> I am ecstatic, and yet... I am taken aback by the relief etched on the doctor's face. Did he really think the chemo might not work? He never seemed uncertain before. Is anything not certain in this battle? I'm getting choked up, fighting back tears. David and I do a light hand slap. I lock on Laura's eyes. Nothing needs to be said. We nod at each other and savor the moment. The relief on David's face says it all. It is time to celebrate.

CHAPTER 6

Cancer is an insidious presence. It enters a home, uninvited, bringing pain, chaos and constant disruption of a family's most cherished dreams and plans. It listens in on every conversation, taunting, threatening, refusing to be dislodged easily. Our joy over the success of David's first cycle of cancer treatment was tempered by the knowledge that the enemy was not completely gone.

Once more, David was towing his computerized equipment, Cytoxin was flowing into him, and the exuberance we had all felt just a few days earlier gave way to the blahs. And that's when the phone rang with the news of a visit from members of the Texas A&M football team.

The timing was perfect. Brandon, Terrence, Tydrick and Chad arrived with all the enthusiasm healthy young college athletes carry with them wherever they go. Tom and I joined them in the family room and listened as David answered their questions, sketching his cancer regimen for them, but that's not what he wanted to talk about. David was hungry for news about the team, about their schedule, about campus activities.

Texas A&M University is a school of great tradition. The fall season, with the Midnight Yells, football games and marching Corps of Cadets, and other long-held customs can make a believer out of an otherwise nonchalant observer. Kids like David, and these football players, become avid devotees of everything "Aggie." The boys could have talked for hours about all the excitement on campus, but in the end, the conversation turned to faith: David's.

It seemed the campus buzzed with news about David, they said. People were praying for him, wishing him well, and marveling at the strength of his faith during this painful time.

These friends knew it was more than just an abstract faith, more than merely a positive outlook. They knew his faith was authentic; that it was durable; that it was centered in the certainty of a living, loving, knowable God.

As the players got ready to leave, Tom said, "I'd like to pray before you go."

We all stood together in a circle and Tom thanked God for these faithful young men and for the time they took to stop and see David. He prayed for their safety on the football field, and then he prayed for David.

"Father, we know our David is facing *his* Goliath. It's a mighty battle, and he needs You. Give him courage and strength to fight on."

Over the next weeks, it seemed that prayer was ever-present in our thoughts.

David's tough chemo regimen caused the miserable side effects to last longer. His feel-good days were fewer and farther between. David began to feel discouraged. His best days were the weekends, when college football reigned supreme on television. Whether he was at the hospital for a transfusion or at home attached to his computer system of chemo drugs, a college football game made the time more bearable.

Always, David's mind and heart were on college life. His friends were heading back to College Station, settling in for their sophomore year. Back in the spring, before David's accident and the diagnosis, Tom and I had helped David move furniture into a house he planned to share with his friends, Joseph, Joe and Peter, at 1102 Village Street. The boys called it simply "1102". That's where David desperately wanted to be.

Joseph, Joe, and Peter were each from a family of three sons, each of a different birth order. Maybe that's why they gravitated toward one another. They were all passionate about A&M sports. They had turned the living room at 1102 into a home theatre dominated by a large television screen for watching games and entertaining. Only one thing was missing: David. His bedroom was left without a tenant, but they refused to let anyone take his space. They paid his rent, over our resistance, and insisted that his bedroom was waiting for him, at least for a weekend visit.

As Jon packed up and returned to A&M for his senior year, I felt his loss terribly. I hated seeing him leave, and I knew David was wishing he could go as well.

Andrew resumed school activities too, starting his sophomore year of high school. He turned sixteen and passed his driver's test, so he began driving himself to school. It was a mixed blessing: I was glad he could get out the door by himself every morning, but I worried about his safety on the road. He was playing varsity golf and would move on to basketball as soon as the season started. He would be leaving early and staying late every day.

I struggled with anxiety about all my children. David's health was a never-ending, never-lessening concern. Jon was entering the final months of his college career, and I wanted to have enough energy and enthusiasm to support him. And I desperately wanted to be available and attentive to my youngest son. I wanted to be engaged in his life. Tom and I talked with him about how we could do that, given the extraordinary demands of David's cancer.

We committed with Andrew to attend every event, PTA meeting, golf tournament and basketball game that we possibly could. We *had* to be attentive to Andrew and all the emotional pain he was experiencing as a sensitive 16-year-old. Along with Jon, Andrew had helped us care for David over the summer months. He had watched his brother suffer and stepped in to do things that, under normal circumstances, I would have never asked of a teenager. He had been forced to mature in unexpected ways, and I wanted to be sure his own emotional needs were not being ignored.

We would do our best for all three of our sons, but God would have to supply the energy and strength for us.

David's friends, at A&M and elsewhere, stayed in close contact with him through the internet. Hundreds of messages showed up on Facebook, addressed to "Gilby", his nickname. Jon set David up at the Caringbridge website where postings showed up by the dozens every day. When David felt like it, he responded, without having to talk—talking took energy he didn't have and clued Tom and me in on just how bad he felt. The worse the chemo side effects, the more quiet and withdrawn David became.

We noticed one day, suddenly, that David was completely bald. Even his eyebrows were victims of chemo's harsh effects. His weight was in the low 140's and his clothes hung loosely on his tall frame. His immune system was so depressed that even a minor scuffle with a footstool or furniture arm left a deep bruise, so he walked slowly, cautiously.

He could not read—it hurt his eyes. Action-packed movies were difficult to watch, but he found a few that weren't too uncomfortable. He often laid in bed and watched movies on a small laptop DVD player his Aunt Linda and Uncle Rick gave him, but only when college football wasn't on TV. He still passed time working jigsaw puzzles and working on "Word Finds" from his bed. And he loved music. He listened to contemporary Christian and other types of music and had lots of CD's to choose from. They all seemed to be able to encourage him.

I wouldn't have blamed David if he had given in to his misery and complained, but he didn't. He discovered what he could tolerate doing when he felt poorly, and he did those things. He seemed to withdraw into himself, almost as though hibernating. How I yearned to know what thoughts played in his mind during those times of quietness and solitude. I always saw his Bible open, and that comforted me. I believed God was encouraging him, working in his life in a powerful way to impart as much peace and comfort as he needed for each day.

The days were long and difficult. With the side effects lasting longer, David required more transfusions of blood and platelets. He received injections that worked to jump-start his body's ability to produce healthy blood cells by stimulating the marrow. The farther we went in his treatment plan, the longer it took for his body to respond to these shots. The blood and platelet transfusions came more often.

I spoke with Judy and Dr. Firstenberg about organizing a blood drive to give in return and assist with David's supply. I sent out a mass email to family and friends with the urgent request for anyone who could to please donate blood and/or platelets. It was especially important for those with David's specific blood type, O+, but I encouraged everyone to donate. Blood and platelets were always needed.

My inbox was flooded with emails and phone calls responding to the request. I began working with Carter Blood Care to put together a list of Donor Friends. Six arrived immediately to donate: Melissa and Megan, Gloria, Martha, Jay, and Stacey. Many others continued to donate as credit to David. People who loved David and our family said they were so glad to finally be able to do something tangible to help us, while at the same time replenishing the blood supply for others in need.

Tom and I donated blood as often as we were allowed to. We made time to go to the blood center and sit for as long as it took, even though time, for us, was scarce. We viewed it as a win-win situation: it made us feel good—we were actively, tangibly helping David; and it was a way for all of us as a family to acknowledge God's grace and mercy. Many others did the same.

Autumn was ablaze with God's grace and mercy for our family. Daily I was aware of His intimate presence. Certain moments stood out as dramatic evidence that He was aware of our need for Him and ready and willing to be strong in the face of our weakness. One of those moments occurred when we met Meg Brown. Our friend Steve heard her speak at a Rotary Club meeting in Arlington and learned that she had battled the same kind of non-Hodgkins lymphoma that David was fighting. Steve caught up with her after the meeting and told her about David. Meg called our home a few days later and the next week she came over for dinner. We were excited to spend time with this young woman who was doing so well in her recovery. A special friendship began the evening we ate lasagna together and listened to her remarkable story.

As a senior UT basketball player for the Lady Longhorns, Meg had suffered symptoms and grown weak while an undetected mass grew around her esophagus. For months her condition worsened until it was finally diagnosed as non-Hodgkins lymphoma. By that time, her cancer was already at stage four, and Meg was just hours from death. When we met her she was recuperating from a successful stem cell transplant. She was doing well and, though stiff and moving slowly, her prognosis was excellent.

That evening over dinner, Meg and David connected over more than just their cancer. Their shared passion for basketball and their strong, competitive spirits made them instant friends as well as lively rivals: she a Longhorn and he an Aggie. Their conversation bounced back and forth with teasing challenges only a Texan can understand, but they were in agreement about their desire to beat cancer and live fully.

Meg phoned one day and invited David to be one of the Honored Heroes for the Leukemia-Lymphoma Society, North Texas Chapter. He was overwhelmed.

"It will be a privilege," he told her.

The four of us attended the fall ceremony together. It was one of many heartfelt experiences that kept giving me strength to keep on trusting God. I thanked God often for the many people who were praying for us, encouraging us: people like Steve, who took time to meet with Meg and tell her about David; and Meg, who offered David her friendship and the grace of shared experience. All these gifts were not lost on me; I was aware and thankful and continually in awe of the kindness of good people.

Caring for David and staying on top of Andrew's academic and athletic demands at school kept Tom and me very busy. Andrew curtailed social time with his friends, excluding himself willingly from many activities simply because he wanted to be home with us when he could. I was painfully aware that Tom felt pulled in two distinct directions: his family was his top priority, but he had huge responsibilities at the CPA firm where he was the managing partner.

Each of us was suffering in our own unique way. Each of us was being challenged to make decisions for the good of the family and for David's good. We were together in this battle, but it was taking a toll on us all.

Tom and I made the clear choice early on to halt all of our activities and involvement outside the home. We didn't have the time, the inclination, or the energy for anything other than family. We tried to attend church services on Sunday mornings whenever possible. We didn't have to coax David to attend—he always tried to be there because he truly loved our church. He knew that these friends were his army of prayer warriors. He drew strength from this connection with our church family. We all did.

If Tom and I did decide we wanted to go out for an evening, it was usually for a quick dinner with Linda and Rick or Brenda and Tyler. They were our sounding board. Somehow, our other friends seemed to understand that we just didn't have the energy or inclination for socializing and, as true friends, they loved us anyway and continued to help us in practical ways, not asking for anything in return. They understood that we were digging in. We could not stop to feel pity or analyze our current life storm. We just had to keep moving and doing what had to be done.

We talked to Jon on the phone often, giving him details of the battle on the home front and enjoying the news of his life. To others, we sent emails. It was our primary means of feeling connected to the outside world. We sent updates, prayer requests and praise for answered prayer to a group of family and friends.

* * *

Tom's Reflections, mid-September, 2004

The world's perception of the father of the child with cancer is not fair. Once David's protocol started and some time passed, it was supposed to be business as usual for me: go to work each day, manage the firm, meet with clients, come home at the end of the day. I am uncomfortable with the way it looks, and I am definitely uncomfortable with the way I feel.

My partners at the firm have been splendid and understanding. My clients are sincerely concerned and have said so. Yet, my heart wants to follow David throughout the day. It is an awkward feeling to me— my second son is fighting this deadly cancer and I am going to work every day. Yes, I am joining David and Laura for the important doctor visits, but I carry this odd, maybe guilty, feeling that I should be with David more.

I want to honor, respect and acknowledge David's courageous battle. I need to work; I want to work; I want time with David. Somehow, I must get the right balance in my life.

I am a blessed man—lovely wife, three great sons, faithful family and friends, committed business partners, and concerned clients. The awkward feeling, though, will not go away.

CHAPTER 7

"I need to get back to school and see my friends."

Dr. Firstenberg frowned, listening to David's plea. Could he put himself in the place of this eager young man who was missing so much?

David yearned for campus life. He wanted to go to a football game, see the Corps men and women in uniform, visit his professors and flirt with girls.

"The best-looking women in the world are at Texas A&M," he said, grinning, hoping to appeal to Dr. F's sense of humor. "September 24th, that's the date. Big game, though Aggies have an away game, I'll be at 1102. Lots of fun. I need to go."

I knew he needed to go; Tom knew he needed it. Would Dr. F understand and release him?

"Just tell me what to do and I'll do it," David said. "I just need to get down there and see everyone. Can we work it out?"

Dr. F studied David's file, glanced at the calendar.

"All right, yes, David. I'll let you go for the weekend, but here's what has to happen: every aspect of the round of chemo has to fall into place. Everything has to be in sync. Your ability to rebound from the side effects will be very important. If your blood counts are within a reasonable range and you exercise caution and use common sense, I think you *should* go!"

David beamed.

"That weekend will be the halfway mark of your protocol," Dr. F said. "A nice point to celebrate, I think."

David was ecstatic. He left the office with a resurgence of energy he hadn't had in a long time. He had something to aim for, something to finally look forward to. He loved autumn; he loved college football. He ached for the camaraderie he was missing.

We started making plans. Tom and I would drive Dave to his house in College Station, drop him off, and then go on to Austin to spend the weekend by ourselves. We knew David needed space; we all needed space, I suppose, but hovering had become as natural as breathing. Already I was beginning to worry about germs.

David's immune system was compromised by the chemo treatments. For months I had carefully monitored his environment, his guests—dangerous virus bugs could be lying in wait anywhere. All this began to gnaw at me as I thought about David's weekend with his college friends.

I wanted to be excited and hopeful. I wanted to enter into his joy and celebrate this oasis in the desert of his disease. But what if he didn't sleep enough? What if he didn't eat right? What if he succumbed to some nasty infection that his weakened body couldn't fend off?

Breathe, I told myself. *Breathe, and pray.*

Someone once said, "Let go or get dragged." I could feel myself being dragged. It was time to let go.

One day at a time, I thought. *I will trust God one day at a time.*

September in Texas is usually hot, and folks get testy about it, but this year my family didn't care that the temperatures were still near a hundred every day. Fall brought us a new kind of determination. We were preoccupied with excitement about David's upcoming trip, but travel thoughts moved to simmer on the back burner when he began his next round of chemo. All energies returned to the battle field. We had serious fighting to do before David would be ready for a weekend of fun. Labor Day came and went with David on three antibiotics as well as strong anti-nausea meds. His weight still hovered in the low 140's as we made daily visits to the cancer center.

On Friday, September 10th, with another tough round of Methotrexate and Ara-C (the red devil) completed, we learned that his red blood count was low, so he received an injection of Procrit to boost the red blood cells into action. On the good news side, his platelets and white blood count seemed to be hanging in there, for now, but even good news isn't an antidote for nausea. David made it as far as the parking lot before he vomited into the shrubs. A nurse came running with towels and a bag and together we helped him back into the Infusion Place where Derek and Mary cared for him.

Watching David, my heart broke. He wanted desperately to be able to do the things that had always mattered to him. He wanted his health back, his body back. He didn't complain, or demand, but I could see it in his eyes. Little things, things that seem so ordinary, so minute, meant so much to him, like being able to drive the car to the recreation center near our house, being able to climb on a stationary bike and pedal.

Tom and I saw him arrive at the center one day. We were jogging the indoor track when he came in. We watched him muster his strength, pedaling the bike. Four minutes later he stopped to rest. Then, he began again, slowly pushing the pedals for another four minutes. Sweat beaded on his forehead.

Sudden rage enveloped me. *Why this child? Why, God? This is so unfair! It's cruel, God, and I don't understand it! Why?*

If there were answers, I didn't hear them. I heard only my own grief and frustration. My 20-year old son, who just months ago played hours of basketball with great endurance—today he struggled to pedal a bike for four minutes.

I swallowed against the rage and watched him climb off the bike and walk slowly to the exit door. Tom and I followed a few minutes later and found him at home, lying down, trying to recover from the exertion.

David's nurses, Mary and Derek, had tried to prepare us for every phase of his treatment, but nothing could have prepared me for the intensity of my feelings that day. The chemo would accumulate in his body, they told us. It will be difficult, they said. We were supposed to know that, be ready for it. It didn't help. I was tired of watching my child suffer. And I was angry. A storm of fury shook me. Hours later, when it blew itself out, I was left with this thought: David was responding to the chemo drugs. The treatment was working. David would head into remission soon, head back to school at A&M, and life would return to normal.

I was sure of it.

I could keep going.

I felt a small sliver of hope slice through the anger. Gratitude displaced rage.

I would keep going. We would all keep going, doing what had to be done, asking for courage to keep trusting, believing.

God was real to me. If I was trusting Him, it was because He was convincing me that He was trustworthy. I felt His breath when I could not hear His voice. It was warm and strong in my soul, blowing promises, anchoring me. He would get us through this.

All would be well.

David and I got up every morning and continued our routine at the Infusion Place. Our thoughts focused on the weekend trip just days away, we both took some renewed optimism with us. Every morning David sat for blood work, antibiotic infusions and anti-nausea meds. On Saturday, the 18th, he needed a blood transfusion. Since his last chemo treatment eight days earlier, his blood count had been dangerously low. If he was going to be able to go to College Station in less than a week, things had to begin improving quickly. The blood transfusion was his best hope.

Sunday labs brought the news that David needed a platelet transfusion. Once again we found ourselves wheeling David down the hospital hallway. He settled into his chair for what would be a long afternoon. Tom and I stayed for while, until Andrew arrived to relieve us. For the next couple of hours the boys watched football together, saying little, enduring more than either of them could articulate.

Five more days: that's all we had. On September 23, Dr. Firstenberg would evaluate and decide if David could leave for the weekend. Five days to recover from chemo's deadly work. Early tests showed his blood counts making a slow ascent, but the trip would remain an uncertainty until Dr. F signed off on it. Until Thursday, we could only hope and pray.

The waiting was painful, interrupted by phone calls and emails from David's friends, and his brother Jon, all sending him encouragement and telling him they were praying for him, couldn't wait for his visit. Tom and I tried to show optimism. We tried to believe David would recover enough to get Dr. Firstenberg's okay for his trip, but it wasn't easy. His energy depleted, his spirits had begun to tumble. He was weak, and for the first time, sullen. The air in our home crackled with tension: David worried and stressed about not being able to go, while I agonized over whether he would survive if Dr. F let him go.

Would he have the energy and strength to hang out with college kids for an entire weekend? Would 1102 Village be a safe place for him? Would his unoccupied room, held in trust for him by his friends, be germ-free enough for him to stay there safely?

As Thursday approached, my anxiety soared.

Lord, you've got to help me trust You.

Once more, God gave me reason to hang on. The doctors called with the news that David didn't need any more spinal taps. The last of those horrific procedures was history; he no longer needed chemo injected into his spine. We celebrated, letting ourselves laugh again, letting ourselves hope.

Thursday afternoon, September 23rd, *finally* arrived and I could sense Dave's anxiety as we drove to his appointment. Dr. F examined him, studied his chart, discussed his blood counts, and asked David how he felt at that moment.

"Good. I feel good," David said.

He did feel better, I knew, but he would have said anything to get Dr. F's okay for the trip.

Dr. F paused, considered, then said, "I think it will be fine for you to go away for the weekend."

David grinned.

Dr. F put up his hand. "Wait—listen up, David. Your blood counts are still low, but not in the danger zone. They're coming up, so I'm encouraged, but you have to use common sense. I don't want you in small spaces with groups of friends—keep a distance. Keep taking your medications, understand?"

David, still grinning, nodded.

"Go. Have a good time."

"Thank you, thank you! You don't know how much I want this. I'm so ready to go, even for just two days. I'll be careful," he promised.

He was already up and moving toward the door. Waving over his shoulder, he said, "See you Monday morning."

Dr Firstenberg smiled. I cried.

We would leave the following morning. David would join his Aggie friends, and Tom and I would spend time alone in Austin. I would put away my spiral notebook and vow not to think about cancer protocol for 48 hours. The plan was in place. We hadn't yet left the doctor's office when I felt fear take me in its grip. Mentally, I began listing all the cleaning supplies I would need to sanitize that room in College Station before I let David unpack for the weekend.

How could I leave him there? "What if's" tortured me as we drove home from Dr. F's office. What if he pushed himself too hard, became ill with something his depleted immune system couldn't fight off? What if he failed to take his all-important meds?

What if this weekend with college friends was his undoing? What if all the progress of the past four months could be suddenly wiped out in one weekend of campus fun?

I wanted this for David—I really did. I believed his soul needed it, like his body needed chemo. And I wanted this for Tom and me. We were exhausted. We needed a respite. The timing was perfect: the halfway point in David's treatment plan. What could be more perfect?

But still, I was afraid.

I took a deep breath.

I reminded myself of God's promise to match His strength to my weakness. And I remembered his friends at 1102 Village had promised to clean house before David arrived.

Help me trust You, Lord, I prayed. *And help Joe, Peter and Joseph to do a thorough job of cleaning before we get there!*

By the time we were in the car, driving south to College Station, God had given me peace. And joy. I was excited. How could I not be, seeing David's happiness? And I was comforted knowing that Jon would be around during the weekend, enjoying his brother, bringing Stephanie by to hang out with him. We were as close as the phone, and I knew Jon wouldn't hesitate to call if there was a good reason, but I also knew he wanted this to be as normal as possible for David. He wouldn't hover. He would savor the time they would have together on campus. What more could I have hoped for?

Jon called us Saturday to report that David was in his natural element. He was feeling good and having fun.

"Stephanie and I went to the house to see him tonight," Jon said. "The place was packed with his friends. It was weird—we had to get in line to see my own brother! He was hugging all his friends, having a great time."

Hugging!

What about doctor's orders to stay out of small spaces with friends? What about keeping your distance? I should have insisted he wear a mask!

Fear flared up inside me, and then, just as quickly, God's peace tamped it down. I felt God steady my heart, once again, anchoring me, loving me.

Have fun, David.

* * *

Tom's Reflections, September 24, 2004

I am so happy for David. I have no doubts about his stamina right now. He is so pumped he could probably last a week in College Station.

Laura and I need this break, too. I know our conversations over the weekend will eventually move toward David and lymphoma, but we will enjoy the different surroundings. Since Jon was eight years old and David was five, Laura and I have gotten away for three or four days every September or October. I guess this trip to Austin will have to suffice for this fall.

We're heading to 6th Street. We'll find a place to sit, people watch, maybe unwind. David's having a good time. Laura and I will, too.

CHAPTER 8

"This guy's beating the hell out of cancer."

That's how David's friends introduced him at the Fish Aides retreat Friday night. His buddy Joe didn't waste any time making good on a promise he'd made: if David could make the trip, he could have first pick of all the freshmen girls. And there was no better place to find a great looking gal than A&M's Fish Aides retreat. When the guys showed up there, Joe said, "Go ahead, David, take your pick."

Bald, grinning, David was irresistible. The crowd around him cheered and laughed, waiting to see what would happen next.

David knew who he wanted to meet: Jennifer. Her brother, Jay, was a great friend and had mentioned Jenn's name to him on several occasions, telling David she was praying for him. David recognized her before she could introduce herself to him.

"You're Jennifer Leftwich—Jay's sister! That's a Leftwich smile if I've ever seen one!" The Gilbert charm was on full throttle.

Of course she would go on a date with him. Of course they would become important to each other. The connection they felt that evening in the parking lot would grow strong and precious to them both. It was the beginning of a sweet and sturdy friendship.

While David was enjoying campus activities and Jon was watching his back, Andrew was with my sister's family, hanging out with his cousins Ben and Sam. It seemed there was no reason for Tom and me to do anything more than rest and relax. We settled into our hotel in Austin, determined to try and clear our heads and capture the ambiance of Austin.

We found a trail near the hotel and went fast-walking. Deep in conversation, we got lost on the way back, meandering far off course, but we didn't mind. We both knew we needed all the sunshine and exercise we could get.

For a while, I was able to delete thoughts of David hugging and being hugged, sharing germs and staying up too late at night. I knew David had left his concerns behind in Arlington, and for this short time, the morale boost he was getting was more important to his well-being than meticulous caution. So I was willing to leave my concerns behind too, at least for a few hours.

Hope was like a living presence among us that weekend: Tom and I, willing to hope that David would soon be back at school as a full-time student; and David, of course, hoping that he would be able to regain his life and resume the normal pleasures and pursuits of a young man. Somehow, each of us—David in College Station and Tom and I in Austin—enjoyed the sweet movement of hope through our souls.

For that brief weekend, our family regained a kind of normalcy. How good it felt. Tom and I let ourselves reminisce about the days when the boys were younger. We shared laughs, and some tears, over precious memories from their births to Little League days, to golf and basketball as teenagers. We recalled how each one fell in love with basketball as early as about five years old. But with golf, although Tom had instructed them in the basics of the game at a young age, it didn't take hold until each of the boys reached about twelve or fourteen. By high school, they all played golf and basketball. It turned out well for Tom—he cherished his time with them, whether on the basketball court or on the golf course.

Our family had always centered summer vacations around golf or some major sporting event. I was the designated spectator and enthusiastic supporter of all things athletic. As a family, we went to the '96 Olympics in Atlanta. And in 2000, when Jon graduated from high school, we surprised him with a family trip to St. Andrew's, Scotland, for the British Open. Three years later, for David's graduation gift, we went to Pebble Beach, California.

The memories kept rolling. Tom and I talked about how excited David had been about playing Pebble Beach. He played some good golf, too, making three birdies and shooting a seventy-eight. Jon played well too, shooting in the low eighty's. Tom and Andrew were not as fortunate, but for all of us, the trip was pure joy. I cheered, took photos and shot video, reveling in the joy of my sons and my husband. Their camaraderie as a foursome on the golf course was something very special to see. It had developed over the years, through sibling rivalries, diverse temperaments, until finally they were comfortable and natural together, competing as sportsmen, relating as friends as well as family. Laughing at each other, losing tempers in the heat of competition—they were all fiercely competitive—they cut slack only for Andrew until his game could catch up to theirs.

David was always intense about sports. His temper sometimes got the better of him. He and Jon played golf together in a match play tournament when they were fifteen and seventeen. David was hitting the ball poorly. Growing more and more frustrated, he exploded in rage when yet another ball missed the fairway. With all the pent up rage of an adolescent, he swung his club at his golf bag, bending his club and damaging his bag. With his brother there to witness his tantrum, David had no place to hide. Tom pulled him out of the tournament and required him to work to replace his damaged club and golf bag. The magnitude of the consequences of his actions made a deep impression on David—and on Andrew, who was always watching and learning from his big brothers.

Tom and I laughed at the memory of David's temper while we enjoyed dinner at a favorite outdoor café on a street in Austin. Savoring the warmth of the evening, the hum of people and music around us, we reminisced about crazy times, the chaotic and challenging times. It was fun to think about how David had grown and matured. We found comfort in reminding ourselves that he had always been a quick study, although he often had to learn the hard way. But he was tough-minded, we knew. And he was a fighter. He was not a quitter. If cancer could have been defeated solely by strength of mind, David would have long ago eradicated it.

Our weekend respite ended too soon. Monday morning, back in Arlington, we had to once again deal with the realities of cancer. Like always, when I entered the small patient room in Dr. F's office, I gazed out the window and watched the cars on the street. The world seemed to be hurrying by. Somehow, that always seemed to surprise me. And even more surprising was the incongruous placement of the cemetery there, just across the road, in full view from the ugly, uncomfortable green chair in the examining room. Once again, I was struck with the perverse irony. Deliberately turning away from the view out the window, I focused on David, seated on the examining table. My pen poised above my notebook, I waited for yet another question and answer session to begin.

Dr. Firstenberg entered the room and immediately asked about David's weekend in College Station. I felt like gushing with gratitude that Dr. F had allowed him to go. The time away had been like medicine for all of us.

Dr. F went quickly to his agenda. There was much to discuss: David would begin another cycle tomorrow—same pattern as before. Some of his healthy cells would need to be extracted for freezing, if possible. Radiation may be a necessary protocol at the end of the next chemo treatments.

A wave of alarm swept over me. Could David's body withstand the effects of more poison? Would his heart and lungs come through without damage from the chemo or radiation?

Pray, I thought. *We have to pray. Pray hard. Pray more.*

This next cycle was supposed to be "going the extra mile", Dr. F told us. It was a way of ensuring that the cancer would not return. The thought that he might need another full cycle was more than I could bear to imagine, and it just might be too much for his body to endure.

"This should be the last," Dr. F. said.

The last cycle would consist of three more rounds. Maybe David would be finished with it all in December. Maybe.

I took a deep breath. *Good, We're good.*

David's weight was up that day. It seemed he had eaten enough with his friends over the weekend to push himself up to 145 pounds! We were thrilled. An end was in sight. December wasn't so far away. Even Dr. F seemed a bit optimistic, although cautious as always. We left his office feeling strong, ready, and confident. As I drove up the entrance ramp toward I-30, I carefully avoided the pothole.

The chemo round began Tuesday morning on schedule. David's blood counts took a nose dive and remained low for a longer period of time, making him highly susceptible to infections and a multitude of other problems. But we heard good news too: he responded to the treatment plan and the cancer appeared to be leaving his body. I couldn't ask for anything else.

Dr. F projected the approximate dates for having a CT scan and, lastly, a PET scan. He said these would reveal everything we needed to know as he planned the remainder of the treatment plan. We would do nothing to hinder David's progress in this battle or to stifle his ability to remain in remission permanently. These were extremely crucial decisions. Dr. F had an experienced team of oncologists that consulted together. Plus, we recalled the results from the lymphoma specialist in Dallas, from whom we sought our second opinion, and we trusted his evaluation. Dr. F's protocol completely matched the protocol established at MD Anderson.

October brought cooler weather. David continued the chemo regimen. Out-patient surgery was required to implant another port (a Vas-Cath) in the opposite side of his chest for the purpose of attempting to harvest and freeze some of his own stem cells. It was a precautionary measure in the event that he relapsed and required a stem cell transplant. The procedure went well. The problem occurred two weeks later.

David had to have injections of Neupogen daily for fifteen days to boost his blood count in preparation for the extraction of stem cells in the bone marrow. The protocol is tricky: there are only two to four peak days for harvesting the cells, and many variables have to fall into place for all to go well. Monday, October 18th, was the target day for beginning the procedure.

One of Dr. F's colleagues was the expert in this process. He was the doctor who had pioneered the research data, and Tom and I were thankful to have him working closely with us. Tom and I believed freezing David's own stem cells was the best and right thing to do for David, but the pieces of the time puzzle didn't come together as they should have. Stem cell technicians were able to collect only 10% of the healthy cells they needed the first day. They tried again on the second day, which should have been peak time, but already David's counts were too low and heading lower. The opportunity passed.

For the next week, we had to deal with David's Vas-Cath port. Only partially embedded in the flesh of his chest, it was an open wound, requiring daily trips to the Infusion Place for cleansing and flushing. On October 26 we returned to the hospital for the surgical procedure to remove it.

I tried not to focus on how deeply disappointed I felt. The whole retrieval procedure, from start to finish, had been painful and complicated, and the outcome was a sad letdown. The ordeal had resulted in only a very small amount of stem cells retrieved for freezing.

The day after the port was removed, with two small sutures left in his chest, David began another round of chemotherapy. Dr. F gave us good news: he had scheduled a CT scan in two days and a final PET scan for sometime in the next two to three weeks. This would be very telling. All final decisions about future chemo—whether David would need another round or not—would be made after seeing these scans.

We felt hopeful. All signs pointed toward remission.

Everyday I added names to the already long list of people I needed to write thank-you's to. Everyday more cards and letters arrived with promises of prayers and support. Friends continued to donate blood and platelets, directing them toward David, or toward anyone else who needed them when David didn't. One day a box arrived from Taste of Texas, a steakhouse in Houston. We opened it to find a case of filet mignon steaks from the owners, an A&M family who wanted to encourage us.

Strangers, friends, distant contacts—people from all around the country joined with us in the fight for David's life. They kept hope alive—hope that David would be able to return to college and take up his life again. I thanked God for them.

I thanked God for David's courage. He was a pillar of strength.

He had become my hero.

* * *

Tom's Reflections, late October, 2004
I'm letting myself look forward to playing golf and basketball with David, Jon and Andrew again. I enjoy watching and playing basketball. I enjoy golf for the dual competition of competing against the course plus competing against another golfer. I guess it's only

natural to try to teach these two sports to my sons. They can play basketball in the late fall and winter and play golf in the spring and summer.

Making a hole in one became a point of measure for the four of us. David actually recorded the first hole in one for our family when he was thirteen. I got to witness it, along with a golf pro at Rolling Hills. It was a 130 yard shot. Then I recorded my first hole in one at a course in Vail, Colorado—a wedge shot about 70 yards to a green surrounded by water on three sides, witnessed by my boys and my nephew Ben. The guys claimed it should not be a hole in one since the shot was less than 100 yards. My reply: "That's a bunch of bull."

Jon recorded his first hole in one at Tangle Ridge, while playing with David, Andrew and me. It was a longer shot of 183 yards on hole seventeen. Andrew and I witnessed David's second hole in one his senior year in high school with a 165 yard shot at hole 6 at Great Southwest Golf Club. Eventually, Andrew recorded his first hole in one in Waco.

What a joy for me to witness every hole in one except for Andrew's. Golf is our time to spend four hours together, walking and playing 18 holes, competing against the course and each other, visiting with each other. Golf is our refuge. If we need to shift gears from a crazy schedule at times, often we head to the golf course. Sometimes Laura joins us, but most of the time she is rejuvenated by the peace at the house while we are gone.

I want to play golf with David, Jon and Andrew again. I want to play basketball with them. I want a lifetime of camaraderie with my sons, all three of them.

I feel hopeful today.

CHAPTER 9

For an Aggie, there's no place like Texas A&M University. Traditions aren't just strongly-held customs; they are lifelines— lifelines that connect the fresh-faced newcomer on campus to a legacy of pride and accomplishment that defies comparison to any college, anywhere, anytime. Just ask an Aggie.

One of the student organizations at A&M is called Fish Aides, a student government freshman leadership organization. A place in this time honored group is a highly contested slot. Before cancer, when David headed off for his freshman year, his great desire was to be a member of the Fish Aides.

The interview process was highly competitive. David was determined to persevere through each phase. He wanted this, and he wanted it badly. Tom and I didn't really get it at the time, but it was what David wanted, so we supported him. When he was chosen as one of the 20 men, he was elated. It would be a while before Tom and I understood how precious and valuable David's Fish Aide relationships were.

Because the group is small, tight bonds form quickly as the Fish Aides work long hours together on campus service projects. David worked with all the energy and passion of youth, enjoying every project, every team member, and every relationship. His illness, when it struck, shocked them all. It was inconceivable that their dear friend David could be embedded in such a frightening battlefield after they had all shared such a fun-filled, productive and remarkable freshman year together. They struggled to believe it at first, and then,

56

as a group, many stood out as his greatest cheerleaders, including the group advisers, Bobby and Ms. Nancy.

David's high school friends kept in contact with him as well, sending cards, emails, Facebook messages and CaringBridge messages. For David, when he felt good enough to read and respond to the messages, it was like walking on air: his friends meant that much to him.

One day David said, "Mom, I really like the poem written about one set of footprints in the sand because that is what I feel like. I feel like Jesus picks me up and carries me through the most difficult days. I feel as if I'm carried."

I immediately visited the Christian bookstore and picked up the poem, "Footprints", written by Margaret Powers. I bought some wallet sized cards and watched David place one inside his wallet. For me to know that he acknowledged what I knew was taking place—that we were being carried by a loving God—comforted me.

On a brisk, bright, colorful October weekend, when David was feeling weak and puny from chemo, Fish Aide friends, Joe and Katie, arrived in Arlington just in time for the Saturday football game --A&M vs. Oklahoma State. A&M was considered the underdog, but the Aggies in our family room refused to concede. It could have been a national championship, for all the wild cheering. Just before halftime A&M scored on a long touchdown pass. David leaped to his feet and began flailing his left arm and shouting. His right arm couldn't join the celebration because the port was embedded in that side of his chest, but he poured all his jubilation into a one-armed jab. Seconds later, he fell backward onto the sofa, weak and dizzy from the rush of excitement.

When the Aggies won, 36-20, the celebration really began. Engaged in the moment, David and his friends were able to forget about the cancer, forget about the limits on his life. David was just David, the same kid Joe and Katie had come to love for his passion and joy of life. They took that image of him back to campus with them when they left, and David, though tired, felt renewed and full of life, for that day, at least. Tom and I felt relief. We had noticed, early in the college football season, that the Aggies' sports success had a direct correlation to David's emotions and stamina. He needed all the "uppers" he could get!

Monday, October 25th, Tom, David and I found ourselves with Dr. Firstenberg, viewing the latest CT films taken three days earlier. All signs pointed toward remission. As we compared all the scans that had been taken since June, the latest scan was clear.

It was clear.

The cancer was gone from his chest, his arm pits and the sides of neck.

"What does this mean?" I asked, fearful, hopeful.

"It appears that the cancer is out of David's body, but we won't know absolutely until we see the PET scan," Dr. F answered. "If there are no surprises on the PET scan, David can complete the chemo cycle and then begin radiation in December."

Dr. F turned to David. "David, you can expect moderate radiation for 20 treatments, radiating the area of your heart and lungs," he said. "This is a precautionary measure. If there was a trace of cancer undetected by the scans, it would be burned off by the radiation. It serves the purpose as insurance—extra coverage."

We felt remarkably better than we'd felt in months, but we were anxious for the final PET scan results. Again, we had to wait.

Two days later, David and I were bogged down with incredible side effects of what we hoped would be his last dreadful treatment. His blood counts dipped lower than ever and stayed down. He was pale, weak, suffered more weight loss and became irritable. We were both sleep-deprived. The dangerous protocol, the intensive care-giving, meant I got up at specific times, both night and day, to administer pills, then eye-drops. After eight days of this painstaking routine, the regimen changed to include oral antibiotics.

Derek and Mary, David's nurses, continued to be patient with me as I dealt with the intricate details of the protocol. At the same time, they were bonding deeply with David, encouraging him as well as tending to his physical needs. Derek said he could read his patients' eyes, and David's spoke volumes. He needed this harsh treatment to end.

They say misery loves company. David would have said he just loved company; misery had nothing to do with it. He had always made friends easily and quickly, and so it was no surprise that he made friends with the other chemo patients he saw so often. One special friend was a 40-ish woman named Linda. In only a few short conversations, David learned that she shared his faith in Jesus and that she had a positive, hopeful attitude. Seeing her on his chemo treatment days brightened his spirit, and he seemed to be able to do the same for her. The day Linda told him she was completely through with treatments and in remission, David shared in her excitement, hugging her and beaming. Her joy was his joy. And they believed his day was coming soon as well.

November brought cooler weather and a change in routine. David needed several blood transfusions. I went to work, carefully planning, strategizing the timing so that Tom and I, as well as Linda and Rick, or any of our friends, could donate blood to go directly to David. That first week of the month, David seemed to spend more time at the hospital, being transfused, than he did at home with us. We struggled with exhaustion and frustration. Once again, our friends' unexpected, loving gestures were restorative. Brenda, our long-time friend, put away her to-do list on the Thursday evening of her daughter's wedding weekend and took the time to donate blood for David. She knew the timing was sensitive and she wanted her blood to go directly to David. It worked. While she sat beaming from her aisle seat at her daughter's wedding, David's heart was pumping her healthy, life-giving blood through his body.

Finally, on November 9th, David's blood counts began rising. As his energy surged slightly, mine cratered. The exhaustion of the past days caught up with me. I wanted nothing more than to collapse onto the closest bed and just sleep. For Tom and me, the rigorous routine had been complicated by having to watch David suffer intense pain and discomfort. For us, this was grueling. Now that he was feeling better and the hectic schedule of his care had eased, we were ready for a rest. David, however, wanted to drive to College Station for the football game coming up the next day, on Saturday. The doctor would have to sign off on it, but to me that seemed like a remote possibility, considering the hell David had just been through.

Dr. F shrugged when David asked permission. "If you feel like it, David, you can go."

I was stunned.

David's PET scan was scheduled for Monday, just two short days after the football game. He had to prepare his body for the highly sensitive scan. Would a day spent with his friends and Tom at the football game so close to the date of the scan affect the results? With Tom being his chauffer, I had to trust and give in.

I was worried and a little irritated at Dr. F.

We're so close... Please don't let anything jeopardize a good report, I prayed.

Dr. F spoke directly to David. "Pay attention to your body," he said. "Don't over exert. Have fun."

Have fun. David didn't need any instructions on how to do that. He went to the game and reveled in his time with his friends. When he returned, it was back to the business of his cancer: readying his body for the PET scan, waiting for the results.

Words cannot express the degree of heightened emotion our family felt as we waited for the news that would confirm if David was truly cancer free. The days of waiting were long and hard. I tried to fill them with busy work, anything that would distract me from worry and obsessive thinking. Finally, on November 18th, we drove to the doctor's office for the meeting that would tell us the results of the scan. David, Tom and I entered Dr. F's office. We sat down, stared at the office door, willing it to open, so the doctor would step into the room and tell us what we so desperately wanted to hear.

Finally, he arrived. Finally, he spoke.

"David is cancer free."

The beauty of the words washed over me. My skin felt cool, as though a sweet breeze had just blown in. My heart pounded, and then quieted, as though it had been waiting a long time for permission to beat normally.Tears stung my eyes. I looked at David, at Tom. They were both grinning, beaming. My chest started to ache. And then I wanted to laugh. Out loud.

Thanksgiving will be wonderful this year, I thought.

And it was—memorable, sweet, filled to overflowing with gratitude.

It was a beautiful autumn afternoon, so we posed outdoors against a background of the season's most elaborate colors as a friend took photographs of our family. David didn't care that he was bald and skinny; he bubbled over with joy. We were all giddy with gratitude and relief. The moment was precious. It had been a remarkable year. We had made it through, together, and we vowed, as a family, to never again take the sweetness of life for granted.

The Monday after Thanksgiving, we were back in the war zone again. David began the 20-day radiation treatment that the doctor had described as the "insurance policy", a sort of guarantee that if even one errant cancer cell had been missed, it would not have a chance against this final radiation attack. For the first time in nearly six months David felt well enough to drive himself to his treatments. For the first time since he'd rolled and totaled his SUV, he missed his vehicle. When Tom surprised him with another SUV, he was thrilled.

His independence restored, his cancer gone, David was in high spirits. And to top it all, the radiation doctor he had to see every day was an Aggie too. Life was good. It continued to get better and better. A few days later, his good friend Katie invited him to be her date for the Chi Omega formal.

Katie was a hometown girl, a friend from Arlington; but even more than that, she had shared the Kanakuk counselor experience with David which bonded them in a special way. They had lots of memories in common. David was excited about going to the dance with her, but he had to have his doctor's permission to drive alone to College Station after a Friday afternoon radiation treatment. On this trip he didn't want his parents' company. His doctor gave him an enthusiastic yes, so on Friday, December 3rd, David drove to Aggieland, alone.

A weekend spent at 1102 Village with his roommates and the sorority formal with Katie gave David a feeling of having been resurrected. He began to think that maybe he could make a comeback; maybe he could rejoin his classmates on campus for the spring semester. When he returned home on Monday, just in time for his radiation treatment, his mind was reeling with plans.

David and our family coped with the radiation treatments and got ready for one last surgical procedure: It was time to remove the port from his chest. With the chemo port gone he would be able to shoot a basketball again. And I would be able to hug him tightly without fear of hurting his chest. The day of the surgery, December 8th, was a day of incredible relief.

Next on my to-do list was to make an appointment for David at the Cooper Clinic in Dallas. I wanted an expert nutritionist to help us plan a good diet regimen for David. He needed to regain the weight he had lost, but I also wanted to be sure he got the supplements he needed to help him recover from the havoc chemo had unleashed on his body.

I already had my own ideas about how and what he should be eating, but I hoped David would pay more attention if a licensed, certified nutritionist in a professional setting told him what he needed to do to take care of himself. The nutritionist did a good job of detailing what she thought David needed to do. Tom and I listened carefully, watching David, hoping he was paying attention. We all knew there was a chance his heart and lungs could be weakened by the radiation, and he needed to do all he could to cooperate with any wellness efforts we could make available for him. We knew it; he knew it.

Later that evening, we sat down to dinner at home. I confess to stifling a still small voice inside me that tried to tell me David had had enough of talk about diet and supplements for building up his immune system. At the clinic, with the experts, he had agreed to cooperate; he had agreed to take the supplements and do his best to take care of himself. But I wanted to go over it all again. And again. I insisted on driving home every point, restating reasons he had to comply. I continued stating all the desired foods that must make it into his diet multiple times every day.

If I had looked closer at David, instead of just lecturing him, I would have seen that he had had enough. He stopped me mid-sentence of my third (or fourth) recitation of his food plan. He pushed away from the table, stood up, and said, "I'm tired of this conversation, and this is what I think about it!"

He turned around, yanked his basketball shorts down, and mooned us.

He disappeared up the stairs while the rest of us at the table erupted in hilarious laughter.

Lesson learned: enough is enough.

It was time to let go and trust God, and David, with his recovery. I recalled him as a two-year old, engaged in a battle over food—when he just put his face down in his plate. I thought, *He's still our David.* I was very thankful.

David continued making plans to return to A&M for the spring semester. After talking it over with Dr. F, he was satisfied with the plan to take only nine credit hours. It would be enough, for the first semester back. He needed to adjust gradually. Dr. F would write a letter to David's counselor at A&M, making the case that he should receive all the benefits of a full-time student, though not taking the required hours. If the counselor agreed, David would be able to participate in intramurals, as if he were a full-time student. For David, this was almost in the same category of importance as classwork! In the letter, Dr. F explained the intensity of the treatment plan David had just completed. He wrote urgently on his behalf, and A&M agreed to grant this status.

Not only would David be a full-time student, but the school also granted him permission to take part in early registration for spring classes, as they do for hardship circumstances. That meant he was able to get into an accounting class with Mrs. Barrett, a professor his friends raved about. He was as excited as if he had just won tickets to the Super Bowl.

Our family celebrated well when it came to life events. I knew that such times became precious memories when shared with family and friends, especially with lots of photographs to capture every moment. December 29th became such a moment. We invited Linda and Rick and their kids, along with our friends Tyler and Brenda and their kids, to join our family of five for dinner at Pappadeaux's, David's favorite restaurant. He had worked there two summers and he loved the food and the ambiance. We could think of no better place to be together. We had much to celebrate: David beat cancer and he was returning to college. We were jubilant.

The host seated us in a back corner of the restaurant so we could be as noisy and raucous as we liked. At one point, Tyler stood up and read a funny piece he wrote for David and roars of laughter thundered in the room. It was a joyous, sweet celebration made all the sweeter because we were able to share it with people who loved us and stood by us during the most painful events of our lives.

The days that followed were, for me, filled with a sense of the preciousness of life. I continually thought that, if cancer could happen to us, it could happen to anyone. Never again would I rush through life without actually seeing the goodness wrapped around me and all the subtle blessings that composed each day. I had begun to learn to put things aside in order to truly value time with my family and friends. I understood, with new certainty, that life and health are such precious gifts; that changes can come swiftly like the wind.

I felt proud that, with God by our side, we made it through David's battle together as a family. And David stood strong with all the resilience, stubborn tenacity and determination he had demonstrated since childhood. Our family, as well as extended family and friends, celebrated the most joyous Christmas season we had ever experienced. We entered the New Year with fresh optimism and deep gratitude.

* * *

Tom's reflections , Christmas, 2004

David is cancer free. His chemo treatments are over, radiation is done. David is gaining weight and his hair is growing back. Tonight is for us—the five of us—we are exchanging our Christmas presents with each other. We are loud, silly and full of joy. It is unspoken, but we all know how fortunate we are to be celebrating Christmas with cancer in our rear view mirror. Watching my sons and my wife, I cannot describe my euphoria. The memory of the anguish of the past six months seems distant and dim.

David opens my gift to him—it's a "Noodles" golf hat. He roars with laughter. I think, it's not that funny, David. And then I open his gift to me: a "Noodles" golf hat. We put them on together and everybody roars.

Wading through the empty boxes and torn wrapping paper, we keep laughing and talking as we have always done in years past. I look at Laura. We didn't cry tonight. This surprises me. Tears have been so close for so long, every moment tinged with a hint of poignancy. But tonight, only fun and laughter. I feel humbled and thankful, but more than that, I feel satisfied. God has provided. And I feel hopeful. Only one gift I didn't unwrap tonight—the gift of David's return to the life of a normal college kid. This I yearn for. This I'm trusting God for. This would be the best gift I could hope for.

CHAPTER 10

Leftover streamers from New Year's Eve celebrations hardly touched the floor before David was in his car, driving south to College Station, loaded with stuff to move into the bedroom being saved for him at the house at 1102 Village Street. College life was waiting for him. His friends were waiting for him. David didn't want to delay. He was taking with him not mere hopes, but certainties. He was full of new levels of energy he intended to spend on all his interests and passions, holding nothing back.

Watching him drive away, I thought how good he looked, considering all he had been through for the past seven months. After all the abuse his body had taken, he looked almost normal. He had gained enough weight to satisfy my meal-time hovering, and his hair had started growing in. Soft and silky like a toddler's, the color was a lighter, more golden shade than before chemo. He was beautiful and strong. I was proud and only a little afraid.

I'll trust You with him, Lord.

The next few weeks took on a dream-like quality for me. It was what I came to call "the refreshment of wellness." I felt like I was dancing in a spring rain shower, daily doused in the cool sweetness of answered prayer.

All of us felt new freedom.

Refusing to micro-manage David's life, Tom and I let ourselves enjoy our own lives, and our other sons' lives, as well. We spent more time in bleachers, watching Andrew play basketball, and being present for his other high school activities. We loved seeing him do normal kid stuff, enjoying his sophomore year without the tension of his brother's cancer always in his thoughts. We gave ourselves permission to feel great excitement about Jon's upcoming graduation in May. And, mercifully, we were able to let ourselves enjoy David's remission, trusting him to take care of himself, while being comforted by the knowledge that he would be returning to Arlington for periodic exams.

We had much to be glad about.

One evening David called to say he and his roommate Joseph wanted to drive to Stillwater, Oklahoma, to cheer for the Aggies' basketball team while they played Oklahoma State University. The game was scheduled for a Wednesday night. It would be a seven hour drive, each way. I quickly thought of all the reasons this was a terrible idea. Could his body endure travel, too little sleep and fast food?

Unsure of what to say without sounding like an overbearing, worried mom, I fell back on the old stand-by response: what did Joseph's parents say?

"Joseph's folks are fine with it. What do you think?" David said.

"Dad and I will talk about it," I told him, hanging up, feeling dread.

"He should go," Tom said.

"What if he gets overtired and can't get to class?" I argued.

"He's only carrying nine hours and he's doing great in his classes. For goodness' sake, Laura, he should be able to go."

Tom was right. David *should* be able to go. And he did.

The trip to Stillwater didn't drain David; if anything, it nourished him. He loved the drive time with his friend Joseph. They talked about everything: girls, classes, sports, and their faith. No topic was off limits, not even cancer. At the end of the trip, their friendship, which was already strong, had moved to a new level of trust. It was a friendship that would stand strong in the weeks and months ahead.

In February, Tom and I slipped away for some time alone together. Cruising the Mexican Riviera for ten days, we took time to rest and savor the way our lives had returned to something resembling normalcy. But even aboard the ship, I couldn't resist retrieving emails, just to know that all was well with David.

"He's fine, Mom," Jon wrote. "He's always in the middle of a crowd. He's happy getting so much attention and care from everyone. Whenever I have the chance to visit with him I can see he's doing great. Y'all do not need to be concerned!"

He was right. I didn't have anything to be concerned about. I could relax and enjoy this time away, knowing not only David, but all my sons were fine. Jon was content, taking only three classes, sports writing for the school newspaper and spending his free time with Stephanie. Andrew was staying with Linda and Rick again, being cared for lovingly. I decided to stop worrying and concentrate on this special time alone with Tom. I came home refreshed and rested.

Meanwhile, David was concentrating on making up for lost time, it seemed. He played on two intramural basketball teams, one with just the guys and the other coed. The teams were doing well and his strength and stamina were improving, so he didn't stop there. He signed on to coach a youth basketball team with Joseph, spending hours every week with a group of fifth and sixth grade boys from Bryan, Texas.

David loved coaching. He and Joseph were both competitive, as well as passionate about basketball, so together they poured themselves into their team of boys, teaching them skills—skills they believed would be valuable both on and off the court.

I prayed often that David would remember the conversations we had before he returned to school—conversations about self-care. Was he remembering to take his nutritional supplements? Was he conscious of his body, aware of how he was feeling? I knew he would never sit still. It just wasn't in him to be a spectator.

Energetic, engaged with people—with life—that's who David is, I reminded myself.

But would he remember to take care of himself? Would he notice fatigue and make himself rest?

It wasn't only sports that were filling David's time; he was dating too. Jennifer, his friend Jay's sister, had now become his girlfriend. They spent hours together, talking, laughing, walking around campus together, losing track of time, missing the occasional class because they were lost in conversation.

Jennifer and David could talk about anything. They discussed his cancer, his faith, his dreams for life. But one day, Jennifer sensed something heavy weighing on his mind. She wondered if he was concerned about cancer recurring, if he was worried, or afraid.

"David, tell me what you're thinking," she said.

"Jenn, if the Lord chose to bring one more person to Christ through me and my cancer battle, I would go through it again. My hope is for God to get all the glory."

They weren't empty words. Jennifer knew David was serious about his faith. Since his return to campus, he had told the story of his battle with cancer many times. Invited to share with guys in a freshman bible study, David told them, "My goals are simple: I want to graduate from Texas A&M, marry and become a great husband and father. But more than that, I want to live in a way that will glorify God." He said, "I beat cancer once, and if it returns, I'll fight to beat it again. But if I don't, I get to be with Jesus, and I'll be ready."

I was awed and humbled when his friends told me how David was talking about his life, his cancer, and his faith. He was twenty years old, and he understood what life was about.

In late February, David returned home for his examination with Dr. F. He wasn't overly worried. In his usual jovial style, he showed up for the lab work, the physical, and the CT scan.

"I'm in tune with my body," he insisted. "It's all going to be fine."

And he was right. Everything was good. The counts were all normal, the CT films clear. Dr. F was pleased and David was upbeat. He left the doctor's office and headed for the Infusion Place to say hello to Mary and Derek. He walked in grinning, opening his arms to hug them both. It was a moment full of freedom and joy for all three of them. Advocates, partners in a dangerous battle, they celebrated victory in that special way reserved only for those who have been in the trenches together.

As soon as possible, David drove back to College Station. His life was there now, not in Arlington. He loved his friends, his church, his sports and even his classes. He especially enjoyed his accounting class. He was overjoyed when he made a 96 on an exam. On one trip home, he posted the test on the refrigerator door and waited for us to see it and brag on him. His professor, Mrs. Barrett, was a big reason for his success.

Mrs. Barrett often chatted with David after class. She knew about his illness and his fight to get back to college. She felt great respect for him and, as a bonus, she shared his love of basketball. Her own son was tall and active, like David, and like our family, she had spent many hours watching basketball games from the bleachers. It was only natural that she and David were able to communicate with respect and ease. She not only taught him well, she also challenged him and pushed him to work hard and excel in her class.

It was still early in David's first semester back at college, but his enthusiasm for the field of accounting was obvious. He had loved accounting since high school when he competed in a foursome at the UIL competition in Austin. We were as certain as he that he was well suited to pursue an accounting major. I had no doubt he could catch up—perhaps slowly, for now—even though he had missed the previous semester.

March promised excitement and fun for David. He would be playing in intramural basketball play-offs, and spring break was just a few weeks away. His roommate, Joseph, was chairing the Fish Aides and organizing the ski trip. He invited David to go along. The invitation was irresistible: David loved to ski, and Jennifer would be going, too. David couldn't wait! Only two and a half weeks. He began counting down the days until spring break when he would be on the slopes with Jennifer, hanging out with his close friends Joseph and Emily, and reveling in mountain beauty.

For David, for all of us, life sparkled with beauty and expectation.

* * *

Tom's Reflections, March, 2005

I got a call from David tonight. We talked sports and classes—he loves accounting. I can tell he has a real knack for this. It comes easy for him, yet challenges and intrigues him. Accounting has always been that way for me. Could he one day follow in the old man's footsteps? I tell him my business is busy and rewarding. I imagine him working at my office one day—I wouldn't mind any of my sons working at the firm. I let myself enjoy the thought while I listen to David sing Mrs. Barrett's praises—she's an amazing teacher and mentor. Then he shifts topics and I have to catch up quickly.

"I'm dating Jennifer, Dad," he tells me.

He describes her: nice; solid; fun.

I ask, "What do you mean by 'solid?'"

He says she's strong in her faith, and that's important to him. He tells me they cooked Pillsbury cinnamon rolls together one night— just like we do at home. I'm thinking this could be serious if cinnamon rolls are involved. After we hang up, I sit and chuckle, feeling good about David. He's happy, feeling strong—no lingering effects of his chemo and radiation. He's working hard and taking care of himself. I hope I can get to a couple of his intramural games.

And a girlfriend? I'm okay with that too. I want him to experience all the feelings and emotions of a healthy relationship.

David is alive, thriving, learning and maturing.

I'm still smiling.

CHAPTER 11

In David's eyes, Colorado had never been more beautiful. He savored every moment. The mountain air was sweet and the snow perfect. The skiing couldn't have been better. Everything about his spring break registered a ten, or above. Even the trip home on a bus filled with noisy Aggies nourished his soul: he was sharing the journey with Jennifer. Sitting together, they talked for hours, laughing and tucking away favorite memories to enjoy again later. But stalking his joy was a nagging pain David began to feel in his back during the long trip home.

The pleasure of Jennifer's company helped him ignore the pain while they traveled. When they pulled into Amarillo, he tried to stow it away while he met her parents for the first time. Their visit was short. Jennifer said goodbye to David and left to spend a few days with her parents in Lubbock before classes started again. David traveled on to College Station without her. The remaining hours of the trip without her beside him were long and difficult.

Localized and intensifying, the pain in the lower left side of his back worsened. He couldn't get comfortable to sleep, even to doze. And he could no longer hold his worries at bay.

Something was wrong.

At one point, David tried sitting with another guy on the bus, hoping a good conversation would distract him, relieve his worries. Nothing helped. His body craved sleep, but anxiety and pain kept stabbing him awake. He was exhausted when the bus rolled into

College Station, but he still had three more hours ahead of him. He drove home to Arlington, alone with his thoughts and fears.

I read the distress on David's face as soon as he stepped into my kitchen. Moments later we called and made an appointment with Dr. F. That same afternoon he was in the lab for blood work and a CT scan.

"I can't be certain of what's going on with you without a PET scan," Dr. F told us while he read the lab reports and the results of the CT.

I felt all breath leave my body.

"Come back tomorrow. We'll get it done while you're home."

Tomorrow. Good Friday.

Between trips to the lab and the doctor's visit, I tried to pretend this wasn't happening. I tried to keep David busy giving me details about his ski trip. I tried to keep myself busy with anything that would distract me from the dread that threatened to drown me. I did his laundry, cooked his favorite food, and waved goodbye to him as he drove back to school on Saturday.

I didn't want him to leave yet. It was Easter weekend. I wanted him home, with me, with Tom. I wanted his lanky body next to mine on a church pew. I wanted to hear him laugh and joke. I wanted to watch him dive into a family meal on Easter Sunday. I wanted him wrapped up securely in our love. But David wanted to go back to 1102, his house in College Station. His roommates weren't supposed to be back yet; he said he wanted to prepare well for an accounting test scheduled for Monday. And, knowing David, I sensed he longed for time alone to meditate, praying about the great uncertainty in his life.

For me, the next days became a kind of life or death contest between hope and fear. At times, hope surged ahead, pulling me into a kind of blurry cloud of optimism; in the next moment, fear, like a firestorm, dissolved the cloud and burned away all hope, leaving me limp and weak, despairing. I was worn out from the race, unable to outrun fear when Dr. F finally called and asked Tom and me to meet him at his office to talk about the results of the PET scan.

It was just a phone call. An appointment scheduled to talk. But I knew.

I knew. I felt myself coming undone.

My sister walked into the house just moments after I hung up the phone. She found me in my bedroom, sobbing.

"What's wrong? Is it David?"

I couldn't answer. She opened her arms to me and I threw myself at her. My body couldn't contain the grief that assaulted me. I wailed, shaking and heaving.

Linda held on.

I cried until my chest ached with the effort to pull in air.

Linda cried.

My dog George wailed at the foot of the bed.

When I had no breath left, and no more tears, I collapsed across the bed. I tried to speak, but only small, choking sounds erupted. Linda sat close. She listened and understood. When Tom arrived home, she left me alone with him.

The evening passed in a blur for both of us. We cried, tried to pray and, at times, tried to convince ourselves that the cancer was not back. But we both sensed that the past weeks of health and peace had been only a brief respite. We were heading back into battle, only this time, we were going in fully versed on the awful realities of war.

The next day, we listened while Dr. F talked.

"The PET scan shows spots on the lower lung." He pointed to the film. "See this? This is fluid here below the left lung."

I wanted to get up and run out of the room.

"I feel strongly that the lymphoma has returned," Dr. F said.

We have to tell David, I thought. Horror rushed over me.

Nothing I had felt since David's first diagnosis matched what I felt in that moment. The pain of it was searing. I couldn't listen to Dr. F. What could he say that was worth hearing?

My son is sick with cancer. Again.

The life he loved, the life he just returned to, with friends and classes and sports and fun, must once again shut down.

The doctor was still talking. My hands lay idle in my lap. No note taking. No questions to ask. No plans to formulate. All time and space seemed filled with the dread of having to call David and tell him the news.

My head pounded. My heart raced. My body burned like a fever. I snatched up a magazine and fanned myself, trying to slow down my thoughts. They wouldn't be stilled.

Why? I cried from my heart. *This is cruel! It's so wrong!*

Everything about his life is so full! Why is the cancer back? Why is this happening again?

Rage and fear consumed me. I couldn't sit still in my chair. I stood and walked to the window. I couldn't stand without trembling. I sat down again. Up, and then down, pacing, then dropping back into my chair. Emotions jumbled through me but I could only recognize the rage.

This shouldn't be happening again! He has so much life in him! Things are good for him. He's got so much to give!

I couldn't be strong, or rational, or calm. Tom would have to be the one. I just couldn't make sense of this. I couldn't shape the questions that needed to be asked. I couldn't let myself imagine the answers—answers that would no doubt include chemotherapy again. No, not again. Not for David. I wouldn't allow it.

"I want to try him on a new drug called Campath," Dr. F said.

Almost against my will, my mind returned to the conversation around me. I *had* to listen. Tom and Dr. F were talking about a different protocol for David. Did we have any options besides chemotherapy? Was that our only choice? Questions started piling up in my head and with the questions came a surge of strength. Like a lioness intent on protecting her young, I stepped into the conversation on full alert. Focused, attentive, I was ready. I opened my notebook and picked up my pen. I jotted the word "Campath."

"David needs a port in his chest again, and I'll want another biopsy."

I winced as I wrote it down.

For two hours, Tom and Dr. F talked while I took notes. The familiar routine of writing in my notebook settled me, and at some point a familiar optimism rose inside me. I heard my heart tell me, "David will be all right. This is only a painful interruption, but he beat it once, and he can beat it again."

Any other message would have been incomprehensible.

Tom and I left the doctor's office exhausted, depleted. We dreaded calling David with the news that the cancer was back. How would we muster the strength? We couldn't put if off. David answered on the first ring. He wasn't surprised.

"I thought it was back," he said. In the next breath, he went into his joking mode. "So, I'll get to register early again for fall classes, and I'll get my pick of profs and the best class times."

He seemed calm and hopeful. Tom and I tried to laugh with him, but the effort was feeble. David cut the call short so he could get back to studying for his accounting test.

"Call me back tomorrow and we'll talk about what's next," he said before hanging up. But his voice grew softer. The reality was sinking in.

I stood next to the phone, shaking. I wanted nothing more in this world than to magically whisk my son home so that I could wrap my arms around him and tell him everything would be okay. But that's not what David wanted. He wanted his closest friends. Once again, I had to let him go. But once again, my chest ached as though a boulder had been dropped on it. In a vague and distant place in my brain I wondered how long a person could live with this kind of pain.

David aced his accounting test, told his friends goodbye, and drove home the Wednesday after Easter Sunday. He had only a few minutes to unpack his car before he met Dr. F for a physical exam and more lab work.

David's remission had been so short—Tom and I had so many questions. Where could David get the best treatment for T-cell lymphoma relapse? What should be the next step?

How do you describe life in such a time as this? As a mother, I felt like a human sponge, absorbing into my own being the agony that David had felt as he drove away from his beloved friends and the life he enjoyed with such passion and energy. My heart felt as though it could explode in pain at any moment. My brain raced with questions. Fear and dread lurked at the edges of every thought. Again, I wondered, *How long can a person live like this?*

And then one day, shortly after David came home, a shift occurred. It was subtle at first; momentary, but it felt good. I noticed the feeling of being haunted, being hunted, had lifted. My heart didn't feel weighted with lead. Optimism was returning, slowly, a bit at a time, to my dry and fearful spirit.

David would get through this, I thought. And I believed it.

David is a survivor, I reminded myself. And, as if on cue, I remembered my friends who were praying for David, and for our whole family. We weren't in this battle alone. A whole army of prayer warriors stood with us. And God was listening, answering. His Spirit was at work, encouraging and helping. Was it any wonder I felt myself being lifted, renewed, strengthened?

* * *

Tom's reflections, late March, 2005

Laura is struggling from the shock of David's relapse. Oddly, I don't feel despair. I have every confidence that David will win this war with cancer. Mostly, I'm preoccupied with questions about where we go from here. Is a stem cell transplant an alternative? Do we stay in Arlington, or do we go somewhere else for treatment? Sometimes I let myself ask why. Why David? Why again? I wonder what a relapse after four months means. I wonder how much college he'll miss this time.

Now I'm feeling the exhaustion and sadness. I've spent the past few days being logical, trying to plan and prepare, but now I'm just tired and overwhelmed. My heart is broken.

I need to get some sleep.

CHAPTER 12

David's life was on the line.

The facts were sinking in: a relapse after a four month remission was extremely dangerous. Crucial decisions needed to be made, and quickly. Fear, anxiety and disbelief lurked in the corners of my every thought as questions bombarded me.

What should we do next?

Where was the best cancer treatment center?

Questions prompted research, and I found some small relief in the busyness of gathering data and consulting with physician friends, but nothing gave me more relief than knowing friends were praying for us. In response to an email we sent, friends formed a prayer chain, linking together to continually talk to God on our behalf. That, above everything, brought quietness to my heart. The enormous pressure to find answers, find treatment, find healing pressed down on me at times until I felt as though I was being crushed by an avalanche. During those times, just knowing friends were praying helped me breathe and think and try to trust.

My own prayers were desperate, faltering.

Lord, You're the master Physician, and we need you.

I'm so afraid... David is hurting...help him. Help us.

Old familiar verses seemed to come to me unbidden. I tried to take time to sit and think about what God was saying to me. I needed to hear His voice, feel His presence. In those moments, even when I could do nothing more than grab at a thought or read a single verse on the run, I felt God's strength pour into me. I felt His adequacy. I felt Him calling me to surrender to His greater wisdom and the comfort of His love.

Left to my own weak strength, I couldn't endure David's pain. My own anguish would swallow me. I couldn't spend my time asking why and shaking my fist at God. I had to trust, or fall apart. I had to learn to be honest with God.

I'm so afraid....God, I can't bear this...Hear me, help me. Help David.

Friday, April 1, David returned to surgery to biopsy enlarged lymph nodes in his neck. Urgency followed him into the operating room: His lungs were now affected; his chest hurt with even a shallow breath. Nothing about the procedure would be routine.

The surgeon's report confirmed our worst fears: signs of cancer in the nodes.

David came home that afternoon with a medicine-dispensing port in his upper chest.

My heart broke.

Moving slowly, once again unable to swing a golf club or shoot baskets on our backyard court, David settled himself at the dining room table, slumped over a thousand-piece puzzle.

I hated it.

I hated the clutter of scattered puzzle pieces; I hated the disoriented feelings that came over me every time I walked past and saw them lying there, disconnected. Nothing matched; nothing fit together. It overwhelmed me.

My life overwhelmed me. I felt scattered, disoriented. Nothing seemed to fit together to make a sensible whole.

I hate this...It's cruel, Lord. I hate that cancer has taken over our lives again!

Inside, my thoughts were in turmoil. On the outside, I knew I needed to keep smiling, to keep acting as though I was certain that all would be well. I knew I needed to find some sense of normal to hold on to. David, as always, helped me find it.

He would need to eat, so I would cook.

He would need clean clothes, so I would do laundry.

He would need his friends around him, so I would welcome them into our home, readying the guest room for any and all of them.

His first visitor, that same Friday, was Jennifer. She arrived with two girlfriends, Paige and Annie, just in time to celebrate Andrew's seventeenth birthday with us. Family and friends dropped by that evening, saying it was time they met this girl who had captured David's attention. Hilarity reigned as the college girls flirted with Andrew, making him the center of attention, making sure he felt special in the midst of an exhausting and critical time.

It was a great distraction for all of us. David loved having Jennifer nearby, and he loved having the focus on his little brother—not on cancer. For David, for the moment, his world was sunny and full of fun. Laughter bounced off the walls as we ate, celebrated Andrew, and enjoyed the company of three lovely girls.

Watching the fun, listening to good-humored conversation, I was struck by the paradox of if all. The good feelings permeating our home helped me momentarily forget the heaviness of my heart. Warmth and love and camaraderie replaced the desperation and despair of earlier hours. I wanted those feelings to last forever.

I loved watching Andrew being doted on by the girls. I loved watching him open presents; seeing him bask in the attention and adoration of David's friends. When some of his own friends dropped by, they were openly envious of his place of honor among these "older women" whose gift to him was a framed picture of all three of them—gorgeous girls to keep on his desk, with the reminder: "Don't forget us!" The envy of Andrew's friends was probably his best gift.

Amid the backdrop of heaviness and uncertainties, it was a weekend of joy and encouragement. The girls, with their strong Christian faith, buoyed David in ways that Tom and I, as his parents, couldn't. They were committed to praying for each one of us, asking God to give us wisdom and discernment in our decisions about David's treatment.

Tom and I knew God was in control. We knew God had already mapped out the best plan for David. We were just waiting for Him to reveal that plan to us. We knew that, while we wanted to invest every minute in securing treatment for David, there was nothing we could do that first weekend after surgery except let him recuperate and enjoy family and friends. We could take no direct action against his cancer, except to pray and ask for wisdom to make the next decisions swiftly.

David loved the good times of the weekend, but he was hurting. Every breath, every cough, was painful. He needed to be admitted somewhere to begin treatment immediately. Again, we had no time to waste. By Sunday morning, our decision was made. We believed David needed to go to MD Anderson for treatment.

Renowned for its transplant department, MD Anderson seemed the best place for David because it was very likely a transplant was in his future. We were trying to think long-term, and positively, because we knew that admittance to MD Anderson can be a long and difficult process. Our first call was to Dr. Firstenberg. We would need his guidance and help with referrals.

It was a difficult conversation. Dr. F wanted David to continue treatment at Arlington Cancer Center, but he understood our desires and the reasons we wanted David at MD Anderson. He graciously began the phone calls the following Monday morning to expedite the complicated admittance process. And Tom and I prayerfully placed everything in God's hands.

David was in full agreement with the decision to go to MD Anderson.

"I'm at peace about it, Mom," he said. "It's okay. Let's go. But first I need to refuel. I want to go to College Station for a few days."

On that Sunday morning, the day the decision for MD Anderson was made, David and the girls drove down to College Station. The girls would resume classes and the routine of their lives; David would withdraw from school, taking incompletes in all his classes. He wanted to meet with his professors, but more than anything he determined to spend as much time as possible with Jennifer and his friends and roommates before he had to say goodbye.

David knew the urgency of our efforts to get him into the hospital in Houston. He knew things had to happen fast, yet in every phone call with him, he sounded peaceful, calm. It was a strange juxtaposition alongside my frenzied activity as I called to request forms and medical records, tried to secure release forms and, at times, sent clerical personnel scurrying in search of essential biopsy results and PET and CT scans that had to be included in the admittance package. MD Anderson required all David's medical information before they would even begin considering him as a patient. It was up to me to gather it all together in a packet and get it ready for send-off. When it was all finally faxed to the hospital, I felt a huge sense of relief. The first step in the admittance process was complete.

The relief was short-lived. Anxiety set in over the next few days as we prayed about David's treatment, about where he would go. We continued to feel certain that he needed to be at MD Anderson, but the stress of the admissions process ate at me. All the medical information had been faxed, but it was essential that I follow up on everything we sent. It was essential that the medical staff know that David's condition was worsening with every day that passed.

I called the Leukemia/Lymphoma Department of the hospital. Had they gotten David's records? Had they read them?

They would call me back, they said.

I waited.

They didn't call.

I called again.

"We haven't looked at all the scans," someone told me.

They would call me back.

I couldn't risk David's records getting lost or forgotten. I persisted. The department was busy; many people with lymphoma or leukemia were asking to be admitted. Every request had to be carefully analyzed; every case had to be decided upon based on facts and data. It took time to consider them all.

I understood this.

I wanted to empathize with every applicant. But I wanted someone to call me back and let me make my case for my son. I wanted to convince someone—someone with the power to choose—that my son's worsening symptoms made it imperative that he be admitted *now*, that his treatment begin *now*.

Tom took a day off to help me with the follow-up phone calls. He used his cell phone and I used mine, both of us calling, waiting for return calls on our land line, on any line.

Just call!

Help came from unexpected sources. My college roommate contacted her friend who was on the board of the hospital and enlisted her help in moving us through the process of admission. Dr. F continued to help, making calls, submitting data, and pushing for our admission.

I know, Lord, they can only take so many patients.... I know that. There is only so much room... other mothers have sons who are sick, I know, I know...

I wanted to be compassionate, understanding, trusting. But more than that, I wanted the phone to ring.

The hours dragged. Every now and then our land line would ring. My heart would skip a beat. Tom and I would lock eyes, each of us praying a silent, desperate prayer, only to answer the phone and hear someone try to sell us insurance or a warranty on a car we no longer owned. Finally, the call we were waiting for came. Wednesday morning we learned a Russian oncologist specializing in lymphoma had accepted David's case.

In all the anxious frenzy, I had barely noticed the date: April 6th. It was my birthday.

Had it really been only three days? Three days of collecting records, scrambling to get them sent to the hospital, and then calling and waiting, and then calling again. And now, the best birthday gift I could have hoped for: a doctor willing to treat David's cancer. Our instructions: Be at the business office at MD Anderson tomorrow morning at 7:15, with necessary papers in hand; and provide additional medical data for the doctor—data I had not included in the admissions packet; data I had no access to without Dr. F's help. And a final word of information: David would begin two days of thorough testing as soon as he arrived.

I felt overwhelmed, near panic. I couldn't fathom what was left to test—he had undergone every possible scan and blood test I thought the human body could endure, but the new doctor wanted every test performed again. The test results I had sent him, including digital pictures and films of scans, were not sufficient. He also demanded David's biopsy slides—not pictures of them, not written descriptions of the results; he wanted the *actual* slides. While Tom and I rushed, trying to gather the paperwork to present to MD Anderson's business office the next morning, Judy got busy readying David's biopsy slides for overnight delivery.

The clock was ticking. We had only hours to get ready to leave, but first we had to call David with the news.

"You're in!" I said.

For me, it was the ultimate birthday gift to be able to tell my son he would get the treatment he so desperately needed. For him, I think, the gift was doubly sweet: he would not only get treatment, but he would also be in Houston, and that meant he wouldn't be so far away from A&M and his brother and friends. It would be easier for his friends to come visit him.

David sounded thankful and hopeful on the phone, but I knew he felt deeply the disruption of his life's goals. He had dropped out of all his classes except Mrs. Barrett's accounting class. Her offer to help him complete the semester's work online helped him make the decision to keep after it. She saw his determination, respected it, and I felt immense gratitude for her willingness to encourage him.

Tom and I arrived at David's house at 1102 and looked for a place to park among the cars lining the curb. I rushed into the house. I pulled him into a hug, stepped back to study his face, to read his eyes. How much pain was he trying to hide?

The house was full—Jon and Stephanie, Jennifer, the housemates, Peter, Joe and Joseph, as well as other close friends Emily, Katie and Alissa. The very air in the room felt tinged with sadness. Each person there had a deep bond with David. Each person felt incredible pain at the thought of David leaving them; at the thought of David suffering.

The poignant sweetness, the mixture of sorrow and hope, in that room, on that night, permanently marked my heart.

Walking into David's bedroom, I saw his large duffle bag and his backpack bulging by the door. I noticed textbooks waiting to be stuffed in.

Sadness and frustration pulsed inside me.

He's already endured so much pain, God.... Why more? Why, Dear God, does he have to leave his friends?

It didn't make sense. I just couldn't understand. Before I could wallow in the chaos of my thoughts, Peter and David stepped in front of me and held out a huge cookie cake while the gang all erupted with an off-key version of "Happy Birthday."

"Group picture!" someone shouted. We all crowded together, laughing and mugging for the camera.

"You didn't think we would forget your birthday," David said, smiling and pulling me into a cautious hug.

After eating some cake, I met Tom's eyes across the room. He glanced toward David, gave a nod, and said, "Sorry, Dave, it's time to go."

I saw the dread in Tom's eyes. He hated to break up this sweet time. He hated to be the one to take David away from his friends and into the enormity of uncertainty that awaited him, awaited us all.

"It'll all be fine," David said, hugging Jennifer, his brother Jon, his dearest friends. Trying not to cry, they all smiled, tried to say something clever, something funny.

"Don't worry," David told them. He grinned, walked slowly toward the car, climbed in, and we drove away.

I allowed myself only a quick backward glance at the faces that grew smaller, the smiles disappearing. I had to look ahead, and when I did, I couldn't help but see clearly the provision God spread out in front of us. We were going into unknown territory, and yet God had already mapped the way. Fear and sadness had to move aside to make room for the thankfulness that poured into my heart.

Our waiting was over. David would begin treatment at an exceptional cancer hospital, only four hours away from our home, and I would stay with him. Tom would adjust his work hours so he could be available for Andrew, and together they would come to visit us often. Jon could easily drive there from College Station, and David's friends could make the trip without great cost in time or money. David and I would need to find an apartment in the hospital district, but until we did, my friend Brenda had arranged for us to stay with her sister in a large, comfortable home near a lake with a walking path. For David, who loved nature and all things outdoors, this was an unexpected blessing. He would be able to walk, enjoy the beauty; or, if he wasn't feeling well, he could just sit on a bench along the shore line and soak in the peaceful quiet.

I looked at Tom, sitting tall and straight in the car, driving us toward Houston, toward what we had so carefully decided to pursue for our son. His face was stern with determination. He felt my eyes on him and glanced toward me, smiling a small smile, reaching for my hand. I gripped his fingers and blinked against threatening tears.

Tom could only stay in Houston with us for a couple of days while David was undergoing the many tests ordered by his new doctor, and then he would have to return to Arlington. Throughout this ordeal, we had been together, supporting each other, sharing every moment, dividing our fear, doubling our joy and hope.

This is temporary, I told myself. *We will get through it. David will get through it. We will get through it as a family.*

Once again I thought about the gifts of this birthday, and I felt awed and humbled. God had answered our prayers. In an odd way, I felt blessed. I felt God's presence. I knew I would never forget this birthday.

I squeezed Tom's hand again. He looked at me, smiled, silently willing me to hold on to hope and courage. I prayed for strength to hang on and sent him a wobbly smile.

* * *

Tom's reflections, April 6, 2005

Things today are happening very quickly. We have to get to College Station, pick up David and get him to Houston by tomorrow morning. So much to do; so few hours...

Laura and I clean David's room at 1102 while he visits with his friends. I eavesdrop, hear the sadness, feel it in the air. I am comforted by seeing Jon and Stephanie in the group of friends. I find myself entering into some of the fun as they celebrate Laura's birthday, her 49th. It is one neither of us will forget.

Today we will take our son away from the things he so dearly loves. My heart is breaking but I have to hide it. I smile, nod, listen to the laughter around me, masking my sadness, avoiding the moment when we must take David away. Finally, I have to say it: it's time to leave.

I wish I had the ability to share how devastating it feels to tell David he has to go. The room is silent. David and Laura stand up and the hugging begins. Everyone wants to say the right thing; everyone wants to stop time. I hug Jon and Stephanie and walk toward the car, blocking out the sights and sounds behind me. Maybe I don't want to hear the goodbyes. When I turn around to look back, Laura and David are walking toward the car while Jon, Stephanie, and the others stand quietly, watching, waving, weeping.

The emotion of asking David to leave his friends and begin another painful, lonely battle with the cancer is crushing. How David has the strength to leave A&M, knowing what is confronting him, without a single word or complaint, amazes me. I make a silent request of God that I will never again have to ask David to leave his friends and family.

Certain moments are indelibly etched into our minds. Today, driving away from David's friends and Jon and Stephanie, seeing them standing there in silent sadness, will remain with me always.

CHAPTER 13

Nothing went according to plan.

As soon as we arrived in Houston with David, chaos broke loose. The biopsy slides weren't where they were supposed to be at the time expected. Pathologists were waiting for David's surgery records from the two different hospitals in Arlington—records that had to be picked up by couriers and delivered to Judy for expedited delivery to MD Anderson. But tracking was troublesome and time deadlines were slipping out of reach. Unless the pathologists received everything they needed by 2:00 pm, David's treatment couldn't begin until Monday.

Four days of delay. Four days for David to worsen. Already the pain in his lung area continued to intensify.

Frustration swamped me. We had worked so hard, calling, waiting, calling again, pushing for David's admission so his treatment could begin immediately. Now, after all our efforts to comply with MD Anderson's demands, we seemed to have stalled out in the complicated labyrinth of data and details. I could not let that happen.

Once again, our support system came to our rescue. Brenda and Rick worked together, each driving to the separate hospitals in Arlington to pick up David's biopsy slides. When Rick had both in hand, he drove for four hours to Houston to deliver them to us. Just outside the city limits, Rick called to say he was minutes away. Tom and I hurried out to the front of the hospital for the hand-off. In time for the 2:00 deadline, we delivered the valuable packages to the waiting specialists, and David's testing regimen went into high gear.

When David had been poked and examined and all his records studied and analyzed, Tom and I helped settle him in a temporary room, a sort of holding area until a room in the wing for leukemia-lymphoma patients opened up. For now, it was full. So many patients. So many families with hopes and fears like ours. I didn't want to think about what it would mean when a room became available. Would a family walk out of the empty space and go home under the burden of unimaginable grief and loss? Would they leave rejoicing, full of relief? Dreaming new dreams?

What would it look like for us, in time?

Would our confidence in the doctors at MD Anderson be rewarded with a good outcome?

I couldn't let myself think about anything but positive results. For now, at least, David was in the hospital, receiving care. I refused to give in to fear, even though David's pain was increasing.

"It feels like my lung is swelling," he told me. "It's really hard to breathe."

As much as I loathed his chemotherapy treatments and the agony they inflicted on him, I was anxious for them to begin. Friday afternoon couldn't get here too soon.

In the interim, we had much to do, much to learn. Rick joined us when we met with David's in-patient oncologist. When she learned that I was the parent staying with David during his treatment, she made clear her expectations.

"You will need to be with David at all times," she told me. "The side effects are risky. Your son will be in much more danger than before."

I felt panicky.

I reached for my notebook. I would have to be ready with pen and pencil whenever she talked. She would tell me what I needed to know, clearly and succinctly, but she would not linger to answer many questions or offer comfort or solace. She would not be Dr. Firstenberg. I would have to adjust to her style. Until David graduated from in-patient to out-patient status, this woman would be his doctor.

"We have some of David's test results," the doctor said. "Precursor T-cell Lymphoma—only 10% of all lymphoma cases are this type. The t-cells in his abdominal area and in the bone marrow are normal," she said. "But malignant cells are present around his lungs."

The news about how David's lungs were now affected saddened and frightened me, but this was not a surprise. The tests in Arlington revealed the presence of the cancerous t-cells around the left lung.

"Our first goal is to get David into remission and prepare him for a bone marrow transplant," the doctor continued. "We'll be adding the new drug, Campath, to the protocol. It's a protein antibody."

Tom and I exchanged glances. Dr. F had told us it was time to add this drug to David's treatment. We recalled that he had described it as an immuno-suppressant with miserable side-effects. He had assured us that David's doctors at MD Anderson would include him in the decisions about David's treatment and would recognize him as a partner in this fight.

For now, we had to listen to this new doctor. Bending over my notebook and writing as fast as I could, I added "severe chills" to the long list of other side effects we would be trying to counter as soon as David started receiving the chemo drugs. It was all so sickeningly familiar, but I determined to take it one day at a time. We would do what we had to do to get David into remission. That was our mission. Nothing would deter us.

When the doctor left, a tense quiet settled in the room. It was time to say goodbye to Tom. He had done all he could do here, and now he had to return to Arlington, to work. He had to go back and be a father to Andrew.

David and I would stay alone in Houston.

"I'll get back every chance I can, you know that," Tom said, hugging me. "We'll try to make it every weekend, Andrew and I."

"I know." I patted his chest, smiled, tried to look brave, but all I felt was sadness.

Tom was leaving, taking with him a portion of the strength I had depended on every day of this tortuous journey through David's illness. His physical presence assured me. But I was where I needed to be; I had to be my son's strongest patient-care advocate. For this season of my life, there was nowhere else I would choose to be.

The logistics of Tom's leaving were simple. He would ride back with Rick and leave the car with me in Houston. The emotions of it were complicated.

That night, sitting in David's room, a heavy weight of weariness threatened to smother me. It seemed as though a century had passed since Sunday morning when we made the phone call to Dr. Firstenberg, telling him of our decision to come to Houston. Had it really been only four days? I felt as though I had aged a decade in the few days since then. All the calls, all the anxious waiting. Now, another kind of waiting: waiting to see how David's body would respond to the intense protocol designed to kill the cancer and save his life.

I drew a deep breath and remembered to be thankful.

We're here... David's records arrived in time to get started without delay. This is good...Lord, you haven't failed me so far, and I know I can trust You. I know You'll give me strength. I'm going to trust You.

Sometime that night, hope pushed aside fear, and I began to sense God telling me to expect His sweetness to show up, even in this painful, scary place.

Tom hadn't been gone more than 24 hours when Linda arrived to spend a couple of days with David and me. One night, as we were visiting with David in his room, a woman walked in and introduced herself as Daisy.

"My son Allen is in the next room, fighting it out with leukemia," she told us.

I felt my heart go out to in her sympathy, but she was a stranger, and I wasn't ready to welcome her into my own personal arena of pain. I wondered why she stayed, inviting herself into our conversation, lingering where she hadn't been invited.

But Daisy stayed.

Daisy opened a Bible.

Daisy began sharing her thoughts about a favorite Psalm of hers: Psalm 91.

Suddenly, I didn't want Daisy to leave. I grabbed my own Bible and began jotting notes in the margin as she spoke. Phrases that had been little more than cliché to me suddenly came alive with meaning and comfort.

"He is my refuge and fortress...
He will save you from the fowler's snare."
His faithfulness a shield and rampart." (vs. 2)

Lord, You will protect us from what we don't need to hear...

"You will not fear the terror of night, nor the arrow that flies by day,
nor the pestilence that stalks..." (vs. 5-6)
We don't need to be afraid of disasters, disease, or destruction...

"A thousand may fall at your side, ten thousand at your right hand,
but it will not come near you." (vs. 7)
Claim the victory!

"For He will command His angels concerning you
to guard you in all your ways." (vs. 11)
*Even one angel can destroy an army, yet He commands
many to guard me and David!*

Was she really the mother of a leukemia patient named Allen? I could have believed just as easily that she was an angel sent by God to surprise me with His sweetness. Hadn't God Himself told me to be expecting that very thing? Her timing had been perfect: we were in desperate need of encouragement. And in walked Daisy. Words were inadequate to thank her—or God, who sent her to us.

The challenge of sleeping in a hospital room began to take its toll on me after the first night. I was exhausted from being wakened all hours of the night by lights, nurses, and continual movement around me. Added to the physical stress was the emotional. My mind was reeling constantly with the pressure of trying to account for every detail of David's care that was entrusted to me. I was terrified of missing something, causing him pain, interfering with the effectiveness of his protocol. I couldn't allow anything to slip through the cracks.

Around 4:00 am on the fifth morning of his treatment, the lights came on, I sat up, and the room and everything in it began spinning as though suddenly thrust into orbit. Dizzy, weak, sleepy, I felt disoriented, nauseous.

Vertigo, I thought. *That's all it is—just a case of vertigo...*

I shook my head to try to clear it, but the dizziness only worsened. I tried to stand, tottered. A nurse noticed, called for help, and soon I was the epicenter of activity. A fast-moving wheelchair delivered me to the emergency room where, like the other dozen or more patients there before me, I was deposited to wait for a doctor to check me over.

No, no, no, no... I have to be with David!

I chafed with frustration as one patient after another went ahead of me to be seen by a doctor.

I don't have time for this... Is anyone with David, is anyone checking on him?

When finally the doctor saw me, he prescribed a medication that reduced the severe dizziness to little more than a hint of light-headedness. I could cope with that, I thought. I could carry on.

I returned to David's room feeling better, but a little sheepish. I would have to figure out how to take better care of myself if I was going to be able to care for David. It wouldn't be easy. How does anyone sleep in a hospital? Could any mother perform what was being asked of me and not be assaulted by anxiety and fear?

I determined to make my own health and well-being a matter of daily prayer, and I would enlist my friends to pray the same. Once again, I was reminded that I couldn't do this alone, and God wasn't asking me to.

One day during our first week at MD Anderson, a young man with a head full of curly brown hair and a broad, friendly grin sauntered into our hospital room. Justin, an Aggie class of '04, was attending dental school just down the road. He found Linda, David and me reviewing notes when he walked in. I shouldn't have been surprised at this, another "angel" sent by God to encourage us. But I was amazed, and then awed by Justin's excitement over meeting David. He had heard about David's fight, and he just wanted to come by and bring an offer of friendship. He wanted to experience some of David's "amazing attitude" for himself. Linda and I slipped out of the room after introductions and left David and Justin to visit.

For the next hour or so, the two young men connected through mutual friends. Justin knew Jon, remembered him well. They talked sports and told stories about classes and profs and well-worn, well-loved traditions every Aggie reveres. When Justin left, it was with the promise that he would visit as often as he could, stopping by as he biked to and from dental classes. It was a promise he kept, sometimes bringing a lunch to share with David, sometimes showing up with nothing more than his great wit and sense of humor. It was enough. Living out his faith, Justin gave David something enjoyable to look forward to, something lighthearted to anticipate during a strenuous day. Both David and I were thankful.

As the weeks passed, separated from the rest of our family during the weekdays, David and I continued to marvel at the many opportunities we had to say thank you. Every day, care packages arrived from friends and family. Some contained gift cards we used for gasoline, or grocery shopping, or sometimes for a carry-out meal from a restaurant. The practical ways our friends cared for us minimized the stress of daily living for me.

Two of my cousins who lived in the area checked on us often, bringing unexpected treats and reminding us of their prayers. One of Tom's clients gave David a prayer pager. A novel idea, it was a gift that gave both David and me great encouragement. It worked like this: phone numbers were logged into the gadget, and every time someone prayed for David, he or she would key in the pager number, causing it to beep. All day long, and often during the night, David and I heard the beeps—reminders of voices raised to God on our behalf. The sounds became like sweet music to us both. Even in the deepest hours of the night, I didn't mind these interruptions to my sleep, maybe welcomed them *then*, more than at any other time.

One of David's most ardent supporters was Cliff, his friend from A&M. On staff at the university, he never missed a chance to offer David encouragement, something to distract him from his discomfort. He never missed a chance to remind David how deeply he was loved by the Aggie family. He offered tickets to Astros games, hoping David would feel good enough for an outing. One morning he called to talk to me.

"Is there any way David can come to the A&M campus?" he asked. "Coach K is going to be there. I can make a way for David to meet him. Do you think David can make it?"

I looked at David, hooked up to the IV that was administering his chemo. He was pale, listless. I hoped David wasn't overhearing Cliff's invitation.

The iconic sports figure of Coach K loomed large in David's adolescent imagination. Attending Duke, playing for Coach K, being part of what David believed was the ultimate university basketball program—this was his sweetest dream. Years altered that dream, but his respect for Coach K never diminished. He remained, to David, a fascinating coach, an amazing figure in collegiate sports. The chance to meet him in person —David would so want to go!

I gripped the phone, swallowed, and knew I had to say no. David couldn't take a break from the life-saving chemotherapy treatments to ride to College Station, even to meet Coach K.

A few days later, a large envelope arrived, and in it was a Duke poster with Coach K front and center, and in the corner was a personalized message: "To David, stay positive. We are pulling for you!" It was signed by Mike Krzyzewski, Coach K, himself.

David was thrilled. Days later, it was enough to keep him smiling, amazed. I caught him staring at the poster often, grinning like a little kid whose hero just shook his hand.

How desperately I needed every gift of grace God could send me. I missed Tom, and Andrew. I missed our home. I wanted so much for a miracle of healing for David. I wanted so much for life as we had known it to resume. I wanted normalcy, or some semblance of it, and a respite from the hospital sounds and smells and the bustling activity of strangers. That's when the offer from Brenda's sister and brother-in-law felt like the sweetest of all gifts. When David's status changed from in-patient to out-patient, we moved into the guest rooms in their lovely home.

We loved getting away from the downtown area. When David felt strong enough, we walked the trail that circled a small lake in their neighborhood. When he didn't feel strong enough to walk, he sat on a bench and just soaked in the beauty of the outdoors.

Meanwhile, we made the daily trek back to the hospital, reporting in for whatever procedure was scheduled. I consulted every day with the transplant team, excited and hopeful for news. It was an impressive team. The lead doctor was known widely as one of the best. We waited anxiously, hopeful every day that this would be the day the kits would arrive for us to be tested to see which, if any, of our family members would be the perfect match for David.

"I hope it's Andrew, not Jon," David joked. "Andrew's taller, better basketball potential," he said grinning. "No offense, Mom and Dad, but I don't think I need older stem cells like yours!"

David's jokes were balm to my spirit. They were like little moments of joy in a wasteland of frustration and disappointments.

The hospital was busy—we knew we were fortunate David was a patient—but unexpected challenges occurred with unsettling frequency. The lymphoma wing continued to be too full for David to have a room when his treatment regimen required in-patient care. His out-patient orders continued to add more stress to my heavy load as I had to assume full responsibility for administering his medications and monitoring his condition. I was the sole caregiver for my son and, at times, when I paused to think about it, it was very overwhelming.

Monday morning, April 25th, I was stunned when I read David's out-patient instructions, ordering an increased amount of Neupogen to be injected twice daily. I knew all about Neupogen—David had been on it last fall. He had suffered with the side effects—deep, relentless aching in every bone in his body—but that was proof the drug was working, we were told. So David had been brave, if miserable. The drug was supposed to stimulate the growth of his white blood cells. It was essential to his treatment protocol. Still, I felt alarmed at the size of the dosage ordered for him. I decided to check before I administered the drug. I called the nurses' station and asked the nurse to contact David's oncologist and confirm this change and the increase in dosage orders.

A short while later the nurse returned my call. "Yes, it is the correct amount written on the orders. It is not an unusually high amount. I don't know why there was an increase, but it is correct on the orders."

I hated to think that David would have to endure the discomfort of this drug, but I complied with the doctor's orders. I injected David twice, with the increased dosage, and put away my concerns and questions.

That night David and I joined Carol and Buddy in their dining room for a delicious dinner delivered by Brenda's mom and step-dad. It was a dinner fit for a king, but David wasn't hungry. His bones were already aching. He stayed at the table for a little while, picking at his food, then began walking around, trying to relieve the pain in his legs.

He tried to put a happy face on his discomfort.

"The drug is working," he said, rubbing his legs, standing, then sitting, then standing and walking again. "This isn't all bad," he said, crossing the room again and trying to sit and eat.

I was not alarmed or surprised. I knew to expect David's discomfort. This wasn't our first experience with the drug

Neupogen. But the pain was increasing, along with his frustration. The food was a smorgasbord of all his favorites, prepared by loving friends, but he was unable to enjoy it. His pain kept him pacing, unable to sit, unable to stand. I gave him two doses of an extra-strength pain reliever and we excused ourselves from dinner so I could help him settle into the guest room upstairs.

"Try to rest, son," I said. "I'll be in the next room if you need more Tylenol. In the morning we'll head back to MDA. We've got an appointment at the lab."

"I'll be okay," David said.

At three a.m. David's groans wakened me. I rushed into his room to find him lying on the floor, groaning and writhing. I ran downstairs to waken Carol and Buddy.

"Call 9-1-1!" I said, turning to run back up the stairs.

"No!" David cried. "Just drive me, Mom…"

David crawled toward the staircase, his face taut with agony. My hands fluttered helplessly. I couldn't lift him. I couldn't help him. Tears blurred my eyes. I stumbled ahead of him while he dragged himself down the steps. I brought the car around, Buddy helped him into the seat, and I sped toward the hospital.

Rage was driving me. The oncologist had been *wrong*. The dosage was too much. And I had deliberately injected my son with the venom that was causing him to writhe and moan in the seat next to me. He was sweating profusely, grabbing his legs and crying out with excruciating pain. I bent over the steering wheel, swiped at tears, and pressed my foot down still harder on the accelerator. At 85 miles an hour, the route to the hospital took a fraction of the usual time, but it was too long to have to listen to my son's agony.

At MDA's emergency entrance, I jumped out of the car, yelling for the security guard to help me with David. In a few scant seconds, David was on a stretcher and an ER physician began to infuse him with pain medication. It wasn't enough. David continued to writhe and moan, gasping for breath.

"Please, call his oncologists!" I begged. "Call them both! It was too much Neupogen! They ordered too much! Look at him! Please, he needs help!"

It seemed like forever, but the doctor finally administered a potent pain medication that brought David some slight relief. It wore off quickly. I knew David had a fairly high tolerance for pain, so whatever he was experiencing had to be beyond excruciating. The doctor doubled the dosage and tried again to give Dave some respite, but nothing could get ahead of the pain. His suffering was intense, far above what would have been a 10 on the pain chart. No one could explain why he didn't lose consciousness.

I called Tom, frantic, almost incoherent. He immediately left Arlington to join us at the hospital.

Throughout the day, David stayed in the emergency room. As each shift ended and new staff arrived, I explained again and again what had happened, why he was in pain. For twelve hours, doctors infused him with high doses of powerful pain meds that, sadly, did little to relieve his suffering. The horror of watching him, knowing I caused it, kept me in my own kind of hellish pain.

I kept reminding myself, *I checked with the doctor... it seemed wrong to me, I didn't ignore it... I asked...I confirmed it before I injected him...*

I trusted that the nurse told me the truth, that she hadn't dismissed me, or failed to check with the oncologist and confirm the orders.

That left only the doctor who had written the orders.

The next day, when Tom and I met with the out-patient doctor, he refused to acknowledge what happened. Deflecting our comments, he kept the conversation brief.

I wanted more. I wanted answers to why and how. I wanted to know if David's body had incurred any kind of long-term injury as a result of the overdose of Neupogen. I wanted to know if the bone marrow transplant would be affected by this onslaught of white blood cells. I wanted accountability from David's doctors, an apology; I wanted absolution for myself.

In the end, Tom and I offered each other the only comfort we could. We reminded each other that we had demanded to be heard; we had told our story. We had made our point. But it didn't feel like enough. Human error had occurred. Our crisis had been mishandled, but no one at MD Anderson was willing to own it. Over the next few weeks, I gleaned some limited information about the incident from nurses and patient care advocates, but not enough to dismiss deeply settled feelings of disappointment.

Lord, help me, I prayed. I couldn't afford to stay stuck in despair and anger.

I had to move forward. I had to leave this awful experience in the past and refocus on the goal of David's remission.

Together, Tom, David and I made the conscious and determined effort to put the horrible experience with the Neupogen dosage behind us. The t-cell battle in David's body stilled raged. We reminded each other that we had believed God for admittance to MD Anderson. We believed we were here for a reason. We still felt hopeful and optimistic about David's remission and a successful transplant.

We would not give up our hope for David to reclaim his life.

I turned often to Psalm 91, remembering Daisy's sweet voice as she read to me. I looked at the notes I had jotted in the margins of my Bible. I read and reread verse 16: "With long life will I satisfy him and show him my salvation."

It was enough for us. We would keep faith. We would move forward.

One day at a time, I thought. *Just one day at a time.*

* * *

Tom's reflections, late April, 2005

I don't like being separated from David and Laura. I hate it that they are away from the support group that is caring for Andrew and me here in Arlington. We are treated so well—meals coming in from friends, help in so many practical ways. But I miss spending time with David. We were together as a family during the first round of his battle with cancer. We locked arms together to fight. But this— this feels so lonely.

I am so frustrated today. Laura called to say David is in intense pain from an overdose of Neupogen. I could hear David moaning in the background. I am angry. I sense Laura's helplessness. My son is in agony. How could this happen at a place like MD Anderson? I feel like I'm going to explode with rage. I need to get to Houston. Another phone call—David is still groaning in the background. Whatever they are doing for him, it isn't working. Total helplessness overwhelms me. I am sweating profusely—I'm coming, Laura...God,

You've got to help us—bring David's pain under control, send someone to be with Laura until I can get there.

I feel angry and helpless. The drive to Houston is unbearably long. Another phone call—the pain medication is working now, but it's twelve hours after the ordeal started. David is resting. Tyler, our dear friend, has arrived and is with Laura and David. What a relief to know Tyler is there, should something else occur. I should be there in three hours.

The hours are not wasted. I sense the Holy Spirit talking to me. Yes, God answered my prayers. David is resting and God provided just the right person to join Laura and David in the hospital room. Somehow, some way, God continues to give us strength through His promises, through His people, in His timing.

Another thought keeps passing through my mind: This separation issue needs to be solved. I pray for guidance, wisdom and discernment.

CHAPTER 14

Living with cancer is sometimes like walking through the cars of a moving train. You know you aren't standing still; things are happening around you all the time without you doing anything. You can't stop; you can't control the speed or the direction. The view of the landscape is sometimes riveting, sometimes appalling. You don't get to plan the route or the itinerary. You just have to hold on and let yourself be taken to places you never imagined going.

I never imagined moving into an apartment in one city while my husband was living in another. But there I was, climbing two flights of stairs to a second floor apartment—no elevator nearby—carrying boxes, suitcases, and miscellaneous supplies into the small space that David and I would share for the duration of his treatment at MD Anderson.

I made the climb with a big dose of gratitude and a smattering of grumbling. I was tired, but I felt gratitude for the ministry team of a local church who helped me locate the furnished apartment. It was gated and just minutes from the hospital. I would never again dread the possibility of a frantic speed across town if David suddenly needed to get to the emergency room.

One of my first priorities in the new apartment was to get internet access for David's computer and cable hook-up for ESPN. I stocked the pantry and cabinets with essentials—anything I could convince David to eat, anything he could tolerate. His nausea and weight loss were increasing and unrelenting, it seemed. I felt great relief whenever his friends came to visit, bringing snacks, campus news—

anything to tempt him to eat; anything to distract him from the almost unbearable misery of his chemo treatments. No matter how bad he felt, David never said no to the arrival of friends or family.

When Tyler and Brenda arrived one day, the timing couldn't have been more perfect. They showed up unexpectedly while Tom was in Houston with David and me. They offered to buy David lunch at any restaurant—his choice—anywhere he wanted to go, any kind of food that appealed to him. While Tom and I worked on the apartment, trying to make it functional and comfortable, Brenda and Tyler took David to eat, then grocery shopping. The smile on his face when they returned was almost blinding.

"They said to pick out anything that looked appetizing, anything that might taste good," he said, reaching into a grocery sack and pulling out a box of Frosted Mini-Wheats, tortilla chips, watermelon. He was happy, couldn't stop smiling, but his energy was spent and he had no reserves. He was limp with exhaustion when Brenda shooed him out of the kitchen and finished unloading the goodies.

One night around 10:00 pm, the doorbell rang. It was Justin, our new A&M friend who was in Houston attending dental school.

"Pizza!" he said, putting a large box down on the table in front of David.

Grinning, laughing, David picked at it, tried to enjoy it, but it wasn't about the pizza. It was about Justin. The company of a friend was food for David. Together they watched a basketball game and shared stories of school and friends, sports and travel. I fell asleep in the next room enjoying the background noise of chatter and the occasional outburst of laughter. Listening to David, hearing the lighthearted banter of friendship, was for me a sweet gift, a lullaby that sent me to sleep with a smile on my face.

Such moments were becoming fewer and farther between, even though David's friends stayed in constant contact with him through email and the CaringBridge website. His prayer pager still vibrated at odd and multiple times during the night and day, always making us both chuckle. But David's life was far from lighthearted or carefree. He was still engaged in war, and the battle was wearying. His days consisted of lab work, chemo, and more chemo, sending him into spasms of such extreme nausea that, at times, he couldn't walk across the room. In those rare moments, when the presence of a friend could elicit a smile or prompt his laughter, I felt my soul expand with hope and gratitude.

Every day, it seemed, I was reminded that life with cancer is not routine, never humdrum. I awakened every day to expect an encounter with confusion, challenge and, at times, pure chaos. Then one day, I added "startling coincidence" to the list: I met a woman named Laura Gilbert. She approached me in the hallway of the leukemia wing.

"I met your son," she told me. "He was in the lab when they called for Laura Gilbert—he saw me walk up for my blood work and told me that's your name too. He said I had to meet you. We've been sharing stories from the war zone."

The other Laura was battling Chronic Lymphocytic Leukemia. We chatted about her treatment, her stay at MD Anderson. She enjoyed keeping up with David, visiting with him in the lab while they underwent their respective chemo treatments. I sensed her affection and deep concern for him. I was comforted to know that David had made a friend, as he had done at the Arlington Cancer Center.

That was pure David. He made friends wherever he went— always had. I remembered his childhood. He was the vibrant, laughing kid who never met a stranger. And now, weakened and nauseous, he still couldn't resist people of all kinds. A woman his mother's age, kindergarten kids, people of any race, any size—they always had been a pleasure for him. Now, it seemed, they were medicine, as well.

David's friendship with his accounting teacher, Mrs. Barrett, continued to thrive. He studied when he felt like it. He worked at his computer, turning in assignments on-line and getting encouragement and help as needed.

"It makes me feel like I'm still a student," he told me. He was sitting at his computer, working on a project. In that moment, with papers askew and books piled around him, he looked like just another college kid intent on making the grade. I felt proud of him, and sad, too, that my child, that *anyone's* child, should have to work through such horrendous circumstances. If David sensed my sadness, he ignored it, smiled, and asked for a bottle of orange Gatorade®.

David loved it when his brothers came to visit him, and they came often. One weekend, Jon drove in to stay with him for a couple of days while Tom and I got away to Galveston for a short break. Although David seemed stable, for the moment, I felt unsure about leaving him. I gave Jon a list of instructions detailing David's treatment routine. He sensed my anxiety and promised he would get David to the hospital on time for his lab work. David was excited that Jennifer and a friend were coming to visit him on Saturday.

For Tom and me, the weekend promised a respite, if only a short one, from cancer's rugged routine. I took advantage of every moment, resisting the temptation to call home more than a couple of times. We returned from Galveston to learn that Gay, the transplant coordinator, had news for us.

"The test results are in," she said. "No one in your family is a close enough match to be a donor for David."

I felt myself wilt. It couldn't be—we are family. We share similar DNA. How could this be true?

"The donor has to be a perfect match," Gay told us. "Don't be discouraged. It will happen. We will find just the right match for David."

It will happen. The right donor is out there. Don't lose hope.

"The unrelated donor search is already underway on a national level," Gay said.

At that very moment, computers were interfacing, emails being sent and received; men and women in a hundred different places, maybe thousands, were analyzing data, pouring over numbers and codes that were undecipherable to me, all in an attempt to locate one person among thousands, millions, whose bone marrow would perfectly match the bone marrow of a young man named David Gilbert in Houston, Texas.

I felt overwhelmed. The thought came to me: someone else, like David, was at this very moment, living one day at a time, waiting, hoping that a life-saving match would be found. Suddenly, Tom and I were in a hurry to register. Maybe one of us would be a match to someone as desperate as we were. Maybe one of us would be the match found in time to save a life.

Would a match be found in time for David?

Gay said not to lose hope. God said it too, over and over again, in the scriptures I read every day. I found myself clinging to Bible verses with a wearying desperation. Once again, caught up in the grueling schedule of treatment, I felt the urgency of being a positive encourager for David. Sitting in waiting areas, lying awake on the Murphy bed at the hospital, driving Houston's busy streets—wherever I was, messages of promise and hope came to mind.

David and I will get through this... God is going before us and He will never leave us or forsake us.... His strength is enough for us...His strength is made perfect in our weakness.

Unknown numbers of people were praying for us for in that persistent, present darkness; treasures of hope, peace, grace, and comfort poured into my mind and soul. Each day I was granted the strength for just that one day; each morning I awakened to cling to God, to pray for strength, and to pray for David's healing.

The week of Mother's Day was an exhausting week in the hospital. David's protocol called for Campath. Each day his body's reaction to the drug grew more severe. Chills shook his body with violent force. Caring for him was breaking my heart. One particular day, I felt panicky as his body convulsed with chills.

"Help me, please," I begged a nurse. "He needs help!"

Together, the nurse and I nestled David in a warmed blanket. I sat close to him, talking softly, hoping I wasn't communicating to him any of the dread I felt. After a few minutes his chills calmed, his body grew more relaxed and the nurse and I removed the blanket. Moments later, she tried the Campath infusion once again; this time his body tolerated the remainder of the infusion without having serious chills.

I sat close to him, feeling relief, hoping and praying this would be the last dose of this devastating drug.

Mother's Day weekend was full of expectations of joy. I was surrounded by Tom and all three of my sons in our Houston apartment. The idea of being able to go to church together was almost too sweet to imagine—it had been so long since we had been able to enjoy such a simple, ordinary outing as a Sunday worship service together. I let myself savor the thought, even as I wondered if David would feel well enough to go. It would mean a lot to me, but even more to him. He had been talking about visiting a church pastored by Aggie alum Greg Matte since we first arrived in Houston. For Dave's sake, I hoped he felt well enough to go.

Mother's Day morning found us dressed for church, ready to go, until David's nausea overcame him. As his dad helped him into the car to go to the hospital, he insisted the rest of us go ahead with the church plan. My heart ached as my family once again split apart. Jon, Andrew and I went to the service, met up with my cousin Donna, and afterward stopped to get take-home food from a restaurant. David was too sick to eat.

Of the many days that Dave was sick, only a few of them took such a heavy emotional toll, but that Mother's Day, to me, felt like a day of mourning. Dave was depressed. He succumbed to feelings of self-pity. Watching him, hearing the despair in his voice, Tom and I felt undone. This was too much. His pain, plus our own, was almost unbearable that day. And yet, in a tiny, perverse sort of way, I was glad to see David expressing very human emotions. He had tried to be strong, to resist the downward pull of sadness and grief for so long, but now he was letting them in, feeling them, and grieving his losses: lost college experiences, good health and the pleasures of normal young adult fun. And very possibly, envy as well: his brothers were getting on with their lives and he was dealing with his own devastating circumstances.

A few days later, as I was glancing ahead on my calendar, I saw a notation I'd jotted on the square for May 15th: Jon's Texas A&M graduation ceremony, 2:00 pm. I felt both alarm and joy rise up in me. It would be a family highlight: our first son's college graduation. Would David be able to go? When I wrote that note on my calendar months earlier I didn't anticipate cancer hijacking the occasion. It didn't occur to me that we would still be engaged in this deadly battle, but here we were. Once again, cancer threatened to rob us of another event that I so wanted our family to share together. I began begging God to give David enough strength to make the short drive to College Station so we could celebrate this landmark event together, all five of us.

I waited until the ceremony was just two days away before I talked to David's doctor about the trip. I wanted to allow ample time for his blood counts to improve before consulting with the doctor. I wanted to give David every chance to hear an enthusiastic, "Yes," from his doctor, but I had to admit I was not optimistic.

"No, it's not a good idea," the doctor said. "David's blood counts are too low. He is dehydrated." He looked directly at David. "It would be dangerous for you to leave the MD Anderson area."

David was already shaking his head. "No," he said. "I have to be at my brother's graduation. It's not that far. Mom will drive me back as soon as the ceremony is over, if we have to. If I have to be pushed in a wheelchair, that's okay. I'll wear a mask if you say so. Whatever I have to do, I'll do it, but I want to be there. It's my brother. I have to go."

I stood there a little taken aback that David felt so strongly about it. Looking at him, seeing his determination, I waited quietly to see what would happen next. I understood the doctor's concerns. David was still weak. His immune system was compromised. His doctor wanted to protect him. I wanted to protect him. But David would not be dissuaded.

I finally spoke up. "We'll take every precaution if we decide to go."

"We'll see how I feel tomorrow, but I think I'll be fine." David said.

Friday, May 15th was a glorious, blessed day—a day I will never forget. Like a perfectly wrapped gift, the day arrived, bringing me sweetness and beauty I desperately needed.

I was surrounded by family: my mother, my sister and her husband and children, and my husband and all three of my sons. Jon's girlfriend Stephanie stood close to him, beaming with joy and pride. I basked in the sweetness of it all, letting myself savor every moment together. David's eyes, above the mask he wore, twinkled with excitement. The wheelchair was in the trunk of the car—David walked in on his own, sat through the entire ceremony and stood for the photos afterward. The mask stayed on until our celebration moved to a private room reserved for us at a steakhouse. Then, together we feasted and laughed and made memories that will never fade.

"I don't know who's more tired, you or me," I told David as we drove away from the party.

He laughed.

"I've got to thank you for pushing the doctor and insisting that you come today. It wouldn't have been the same without you," I said. "But it was a risk…"

"Yeah, I know," David said. "I wouldn't have missed it for anything."

And then he closed his eyes and slept all the way back to Houston.

* * *

Tom's Reflections, mid-May, 2005

As an outpatient now, David appears to be enduring the cancer protocol, although something seems different with him. I can't get my hands around it. Laura has lost a lot of weight. Is being in Houston, separated from the family and friends, taking a hidden toll on David and Laura?

Last night, here at the apartment in Houston, Laura and I started to watch a movie. Within minutes, Laura fell asleep, her weariness evident. As I watched her rest, scores of random thoughts raced through my mind, but they eventually centered on one major point: Should David, during this outpatient period, complete his protocol in Arlington? Surely the oncologists in Arlington can monitor David and the protocol. We would return to MD Anderson for the stem cell transplant. I know David is frustrated— he feels like a number at MD Anderson. At home, everyone knows him; he is the local guy fighting a terrible battle with cancer. And Andrew and I could help lift some of the caregiving load off of Laura. We could attend church together.

What is best for David and Laura? The thoughts persist through the night. These decisions are made even more difficult due to my tired state of mind. It seems all the decisions are that way now. By morning, I am convinced that we should talk about the idea.

I'm ready for the drive back to Arlington. First, I quietly talk with David and float the idea of completing his protocol in Arlington. David immediately likes the idea, but we need time to reflect and pray. By the time I get home, I am convinced that David and Laura should temporarily return to Arlington.

CHAPTER 15

The side effects of David's chemo treatments were becoming more challenging to tolerate. His body was wearing down. With my every breath, I hoped and prayed that his treatment would end. Every infusion seemed to take its toll. I wondered how long he could go on, how long I could go on. Then, in May the doctor came in with good news.

"At the end of the month we'll do tests to determine David's remission status," he said.

His words were the first soothing words I'd heard in a very long time. Now I could let myself really hope and believe that his chemo treatments would finally end.

It wouldn't be a moment too soon. David's suffering had moved far beyond the physical symptoms of his disease. He was feeling great isolation at this time. He wanted to go home to Arlington.

I sensed his loneliness and tried to encourage him.

"We can get through anything that will get you well again, David," I said, hoping he would catch my positive vibes.

"I know," he said.

"This is where the cutting edge medicine is practiced. This is where the stem cell transplant has to happen."

"I know."

He *did* know. We both knew. He was depleted, both physically and emotionally. Every day challenged what little strength he had. The visits from friends and family gave momentary relief and renewal, but it wasn't enough.

"Mom, even if it's just for a few days, I need to go home. I need normalcy."

I couldn't argue with him. I felt I needed it too.

"Dr. Firstenberg can continue my protocol. I don't have to be in Houston for the transplant coordinator to keep working on the search for a match."

I agreed. It seemed workable.

"Mom, I need this. I want to sleep in my own bed. I miss Andrew and his friends coming in and out. I want to be with Jon while he's there, before he moves into his own place."

I wanted to say yes, okay—we'll pack up and leave right now. But it wasn't up to me. So many others had to have a say in this matter.

"Mom, we can get in the car and drive back to Houston whenever the doctor there says we have to. We can do this. It'll work."

Could it happen?

To load the car and drive away, leaving downtown Houston, the smells of traffic, the noise; the chatter of cancer language everywhere—could we really do it? And our apartment—we just got settled into this apartment.

David's eyes pleaded with me.

"Okay," I said, feeling determined. "I will do everything I can to get your release as soon as possible. It does seem as though this is the one time in your protocol when it might be possible to leave for a few days."

A few minutes later we were on the phone with Tom, discussing the plan. Little did I know David and Tom had had this conversation days earlier. Tom had already been praying for wisdom, asking God to make a way for it to happen.

Getting David into MD Anderson as a patient had been a complicated and chaotic process; getting him out proved to be almost as difficult.

David was not technically part of any research study, but all eyes were on his case because he was being treated with Campath, which was considered an investigational drug at that time. No one wanted him out of sight. I learned that a multi-layered process of intricate details had to be agreed upon among several physicians and research nurses. Ultimate approval of his release to go home and continue treatment in Arlington had to come from a research doctor designated as the Principal Investigator.

I felt overwhelmed at the complexity of the process and the size of the organizational structure that directed the personnel involved in David's care. I let myself wonder how any of these doctors could have failed to pay attention to the dosage of Neupogen that had caused David such intense suffering several weeks ago, but I didn't dare let myself linger on those thoughts. I didn't want to waste any time on the past. It was David's future that concerned me now. And he wanted that future to be spent at home, in Arlington for a short time. He wanted that future to begin as soon as possible.

I learned that the Principal Investigator was the oncologist who wrote David's protocol. I had never heard her name, never met her. When I finally connected with her by phone, it was our first conversation. I told her how desperately David wanted to go home for a few days; I said I believed going home would have some therapeutic benefits for him. I would have begged, if it would have helped make our case.

The doctor listened. She would study David's case, she said; she would let me know her decision.

In the meantime I had to make a decision about the apartment. Should we keep paying the rent on it, even if we were able to move home for weeks? If we gave it up, what would happen if we had to come back in a hurry? Would we be able to find another apartment? How binding was the lease?

Once more I saw God's gentle hand at work on our behalf. The apartment complex catered to the needs of MD Anderson patients. Its lease and rent agreements were structured to accommodate families navigating the path of cancer treatment. Not only would they release us from our lease, I learned, they also assured me that we would have a space if and when we had to return to live in Houston. We could pack up all our belongings and head to Arlington with no fees or legal obligations left dangling with the apartment management.

At least one aspect of this process was simple, uncomplicated. I breathed a sigh of relief. For the next three days I pushed to get David released at MDA. For hours at a time, I worked my way down a list of personnel, asking to speak to the right people, waiting for return phone calls, and struggling to keep control of my emotions and my temper. On the third day, I drove David to the hospital for lab tests and a four hour transfusion of red blood cells. I couldn't sit still and wait. I returned to the apartment and started emptying cabinets, drawers and closets. I began getting ready to leave.

Speaking "off the record," someone had told me that David's release was a done deal. Expect a phone call, they said. Go ahead and get ready to leave. When David was finished at the lab, the car was loaded and ready to go. Moments later, my cell phone rang. The Principal Investigator had decided: David could go home.

I grinned at David and nodded toward the boxes and suitcases stacked in the back seat. We were already on our way.

The doctor's permission came with a long list of instructions. The car engine idled while we sat in the hospital parking lot so I could write all the doctor's instructions in my notebook—she gave detailed prerequisites and insisted I follow every one of them to the letter. I agreed, thanked her profusely, and drove to the nearest gas station to fill up for the drive to Arlington.

David and I both knew we had to return to Houston for more tests in a week, but for now, we were going home. And for now, home base would be Arlington, with our family and friends, as long as David's tests were acceptable, as long as the donor search continued. The plan was in place: Dr. F and Judy would stay in daily contact with David's oncologists at MDA. Information would pass back and forth among the doctors and research nurses. David's care would continue, uninterrupted.

It was the 18th of May. For more than six weeks David and I had lived in Houston. He had fought there, willingly submitting to every test, every drug, every lab procedure his doctors thrust on him. Now, he just wanted to return home, regroup and refuel, enjoy his family, including the family dog George, and continue his battle on home soil, with Dr. Firstenberg leading the charge, in the familiar territory of the Arlington Cancer Center, with his nurses Mary and Derek.

Driving home, I was struck by the timing of it all. David's friends at College Station would be finishing final exams in a few days and then scattering to their homes and summer jobs. Some would be starting internships, traveling abroad, volunteering for experiences in their chosen fields. David was going home to set up battlements for the next stage of his war against cancer, the next big surge for the fight for his life.

He was optimistic. He had fought through the disappointment of having to take an incomplete in Mrs. Barrett's accounting class, but he had convinced himself it wasn't the end of the world. He would retake the class as soon as possible. He continued to enjoy Mrs. Barrett's encouragement. He was excited about going home. He wasn't giving up, or giving in. He seemed determined to win this war.

We walked in the door at midnight. David's smile generated enough wattage to light up the house.

The next day Lamar High School, David's alma mater, held a bone marrow drive in his honor. It was an effort to raise awareness of the National Marrow Donor Program, as well as a time to collect blood donations to type and match for patients in need of this life-saving gift. All hopes focused on David. Would someone in Arlington, maybe a classmate, be a match for him? And would other cancer patients, somewhere, learn on this day that a life-giving match had been found for them?

No one expected David to show up on campus—no one knew he was back in Arlington—but David wanted to stop by.

"Mom, would you drive me? I want to see the people who organized it and thank them in person and maybe see a few friends. And I would really like some time with Coach Webb. I told him I would have to wear a mask and he said, 'Come on!'"

Coach Webb was David's high school golf coach for four years; but more than just a coach, he was a special friend. Once more, I relented. I grabbed the bottle of hand sanitizer that went everywhere with us and David grabbed his mask. We were driving the old familiar route to the school when David's cell phone rang.

"Coach Webb is meeting me in the library in five minutes," David said. I heard the excitement in his voice.

When we arrived, word got around that he was on site for the big event. In moments, his principal, Mr. Jones, came to see him. Then, one by one, teachers, staff, even the custodian, came by the library. Kids he had never met and friends who had graduated with him years earlier tried to see him and speak some encouraging words. David reveled in the enthusiasm of participants, sitting with Coach Webb, as I thanked everyone who donated blood.

Over 200 new donors signed up to be on the national registry to show their support! Aggie friends from other high schools in the area made their way to Arlington for him. Observing all the activity and seeing David the recipient of such love filled me with gratitude for this awesome gift to our family. David wore his mask yet still attempted to visit quietly huddled to the side.

No one knew how weak he was and the effort required...but he needed and wanted to be there. I saw him squirt his hands often and stay seated most of the time. Coach Webb never left his side. After a time, David took my cue that it was time to leave for home. We had stayed longer than planned, but the time was meaningful to David and he hated for it to end. We left with posters signed with messages of hope and love, messages he would read again and again in the weeks ahead.

For David, being home in Arlington, being around the familiar, friendly faces was good medicine. He loved seeing Andrew and his friends. Sometimes he opened up and talked about his cancer and the treatments at MD Anderson, but mostly he wanted to talk about sports. I watched him carefully, noting his fatigue, suggesting he rest, pushing him to try to eat more. I sensed he was willing himself to feel better, and I sensed, somehow, that something seemed different. Finally, David talked about it.

"Something doesn't seem right in my chest, in my stomach. It feels different," he said.

His strength was depleted—maybe that was the cause. I wondered, and I felt wary.

We were spending most of every daylight hour of every day at the Cancer Center with Mary and Derek, as well as Dr. F. David enjoyed reconnecting with them, but he had little energy for anything else. On Sunday, he mustered the strength to get up and get dressed so we could go to church together, as a family.

Sitting together, in the familiar pew in our wonderful church, I looked at each of my sons, at my husband, and dabbed at tears, trying not to damage my makeup. Crying wasn't on my to-do list that day; I wanted to be happy. I wanted to worship and rejoice. My mind, however, wandered. I struggled to follow the message, too full of my own thoughts and emotions to pay full attention, but when I heard David's name spoken from the pulpit, the pastor drew me in.

"David Gilbert needs a breakthrough," Pastor Bruce said. "He needs a match for a bone marrow transplant. Pray with me, will you, for God's perfect timing, for healing and for grace for the Gilbert family."

The tears flowed freely then, with no worry about the smear of mascara that stained my face. I felt enfolded by the love and kindness of this sweet congregation we had worshipped with for so many years. I felt our pastor's love for us. I felt God's love surrounding us, filling us. Looking down the row, I watched as each family member wiped away tears. We were overwhelmed, each of us. And we were blessed beyond anything we could measure.

To be home. To be together. To be prayed for and encouraged by this group of people who knew us and loved us—nothing could have been more meaningful.

For David, being in Arlington meant he was able to spend time with Jennifer, and every moment was important. She had only a few short days before she was scheduled to leave for Kanakuk, in Missouri, where she would be a counselor for the next four weeks. Their last evening together, that Sunday night, was bittersweet.

At 8:00 pm Jennifer's friend drove up to get her. I hugged her, said goodbye, and went into the study, feeling a great sadness in my heart. I watched from the window as she and David walked slowly across the yard. They seemed to be pacing themselves, refusing to rush, refusing to let this moment pass too quickly. I tried to look away, but my eyes were drawn to the sight: They stood together, looking at each other, looking down and away, finally hugging and stepping apart.

I watched the car drive away while David stood gazing down the street. He lifted his hand in a final wave, and then she was gone. He stood there, at the edge of the yard, not moving. Then, slowly turning around, he walked back toward the house.

They say a mother's ear is tuned to the cry of her baby. She can tell if he is hungry, or angry, or scared. I could hear, from a distance, the cry of my son's heart, although he made no sound and cried no tears. His heart was breaking. And he was afraid.

I found him at the dining room table, fingering the pieces of a huge puzzle that littered the table. For hours he sat there, never speaking. I set a water bottle in front of him, waited, walked out. Nothing to say. Only silence.

The next morning, Tom left with David and me to return to MD Anderson for the series of tests that had been scheduled for him before we left. I had many questions for the doctor. The changes David felt in his chest and stomach concerned me. We hoped Dr. F was right: he speculated that David was cancer-free. But we didn't know anything for certain. During the drive we had time to talk and think about what it would mean if our prayers had been answered: David would never need another drop of chemo. As soon as the donor match was found, he could have the transplant and begin planning for a life in the future.

After two days of grueling tests, the doctors gave us the news: David was cancer free. Again.

I felt relief, but fears still nagged. David's blood counts were not rising as they should; he complained about his stomach. Was it stress? What was causing him to continue to be sick and uncomfortable?

I wanted to be exuberant, and I was, sort of. But the new symptoms of distress in David's chest and stomach made me nervous. I was anxious about his low blood counts. He could not be considered for the transplant until the count rose to a safe range. So many variables, and all out of my control. Oh, how we needed Jesus to intercede with healing, with a donor match, with grace to help me keep on hoping and believing.

More than anything, I dreaded David having to undergo another round of chemo to prevent the lymphoma from growing again. The doctors told us this was a strong possibility, but I couldn't imagine David's body enduring that agony yet again.

My prayer was a mantra: *Oh, Lord, please no more chemo...please send us a donor... David, my hero, my warrior, he's had enough...please God...*

* * *

Tom's reflections, late May, 2005
The battle continues. We have been at MD Anderson for two days now, and David has endured a lengthy battery of tests. It appears that the cancer is again gone. Our focus right now is the upcoming stem cell transplant for him.

We are back at the hotel room in Houston, awaiting the call from the stem cell doctor. When the call comes in, for some reason, I walk into the bathroom to take the call. The stem cell doctor tells me that David has a great chance to "hit a grand slam." What does that mean? The doctor says we have a 25-30% chance that David could be completely cured of cancer, then he mentions a couple of other things, but I can't process it all. I can only focus on this: we have only a 25-30% chance for a complete recovery? If not fully successful with the transplant, what does David's future look like? When will this ordeal end?

The phone call is over. I walk out and tell David and Laura that the doctor says we have a great chance to "hit a grand slam." I just can't mention the remainder of the phone call. The burdens and challenges of cancer seem to never stop. And I don't plan to share the odds of success with David, Laura, or anyone.

CHAPTER 16

Home.

It was the weekend before Memorial Day, and we were home. The sweetness of the word melted into my soul as I watched David, his brothers and friends fill the house with the noise of laughter and conversation. Of course, most of the talk was about sports, and basketball games played incessantly on the television. Tom and I listened as the boys argued about the Maverick's best player of all time. One by one, they tossed out the names of favorites who had lit up the court sometime in the history of the Dallas Mavs.

"Cedrick Ceballos!" David shouted. "Best all time, no contest!"

"Naw—Robert Pack," Andrew said. "Gotta be Robert Pack."

"Cherokee Parks!" Jon yelled. "None better!"

Cousin Ben chimed in with Popeye Jones.

Fringe players, some of them obscure, the players' names reverberated through our house as the boys praised them as though the NBA had just announced they were all selected for induction into the Basketball Hall of Fame.

I caught myself laughing; I let myself enjoy the moments of normalcy, knowing that David would soon tire, the friends would leave, and quiet would settle upon us again. And in the quiet I would sense again the nagging feeling that something was just not right with David. He may have been cancer free, but he was still not well.

That same weekend, more family arrived to visit David. Tom's sister and brother-in-law brought Tom's dad, Pappy, on Sunday afternoon. David was glad to see them, but his strength was so depleted he could only sit or lie down while they were there. They cast anxious glances in my direction.

"I've never seen him so weak," Tom's sister whispered to me.

I could only nod and struggle to hold back tears.

Thoughts of the coming transplant were ever-present for all of us. The timing was so sensitive, so out of our control. All the working pieces had to come together in almost split-second timing. I could tell David was preoccupied, nervous. The waiting, hoping, was taking a toll on him. Although we all wanted to enjoy each moment, live in the sweetness of present moments, fears about the future haunted us.

Patiently wait, I reminded myself, looking across the room where David was posing for a picture with his grandfather. *Trust and patiently wait.*

David smiled, and for just an instant, I felt peace. Nothing was going to surprise God. David was trusting, resting in God's plan. In that moment, I believed with all my heart that relief for David would come soon.

Memorial Day weekend was always a time of fun, celebrating the holiday at a ballgame, or a large family gathering that included special friends. At this time, my concerns for David were increasing. I watched him closely. He couldn't quite articulate what was different about his symptoms, but he knew something wasn't right. His stomach issues persisted. He felt "weird, different, the sensations just aren't like it used to be…I can't explain it…"

I was finally able to talk with Dr. F by phone.

"He's been chilled ever since we left Houston. It's like his body temperature fluctuates all the time," I said, glancing across the room at David. His lanky body was hunched in a corner of the sofa. He sat bundled in his fleece jacket, seeming to almost sink into it, seeking warmth that his body couldn't hold close enough. He tugged at the toboggan cap he wore most of the time.

"It's not unusual for chemo patients to be chilled," Dr. F reminded me. "Call me if the fever is over 100 degrees. It could mean he's fighting an infection and I'll want to admit him to the hospital."

Monday night, Memorial Day, around 11:00 pm, Tom and I found ourselves driving David to Arlington Memorial Hospital, the hospital where he had been born nearly twenty-one years earlier. His fever had risen to over 101 degrees, so he was admitted to the cancer wing to fight something—presumably an infection.

Tom and I sat with him for two and a half hours while nurses and technicians drew blood for tests and cultures. Because the source of the infection was unknown, six different antibiotics were pumped into his body. Tom and I watched, dulled with exhaustion and fear. Finally, nurses encouraged us to go home and sleep for a few hours. We hugged David gently; I kissed him goodnight. He was resting when we walked out of his room.

Listen, Laura, I heard God say in my heart. *I am with you, I am mighty to save. I will take great delight in you, I will quiet you with my love, I will rejoice over you with singing.*

The words of Zephaniah 3:17 came to me, personalized. They filled my thoughts as we drove home. They comforted me as I drifted into a light sleep.

On Wednesday, David's second day in the hospital, we still had no word on the source of his infection. Linda was with me in David's room, watching me chafe at having to wait and worry, wondering when a diagnosis would come so that specific antibiotics could target the infection with precision. I was growing discouraged and impatient. I wanted news, good news. I wanted it now.

My phone rang. It was Gay, from the MDA Transplant Department.

"We have a perfect donor match for David!" she said.

I couldn't speak. Trembling, I clutched the phone.

Linda hovered close. "What is it?" she whispered. "Are you okay?"

I nodded. Smiled. Gulped.

"It's a male," Gay told me. "He's willing to commit to the transplant procedure."

Still speechless, I gasped.

"We're tentatively scheduling the transplant for June 26th," Gay said. "Keep me posted on David, okay? And Laura, keep the faith."

I mumbled "thank you" through tears.

I touched David lightly on the shoulder to rouse him from a light sleep.

"Gay just called."

He blinked, lifted his head. "Yeah?"

"You've got a donor—a perfect match!"

David was elated. The grin that spread across his face erased the signs of worry and dread he had worn for so long.

"The plan is in motion, Dave," I said. "It's going to happen."

"Call Tom," Linda said.

I started to call, and then stopped myself. "No, I'll tell him in person, when he gets here."

Tom was working at the office that day. It was hard not to call, but I knew this was too wonderful, too huge, to deliver over the phone.

God had answered our prayers! David was going to get the transplant!

When Tom arrived, our joy multiplied as I repeated everything Gay told me.

The donor was preparing for the procedure. Now David had to get ready. His blood counts had to improve; the antibiotics had to kill the infection.

We were excited, hopeful—the future looked exciting. But we had to stay in the present; we had to keep focused on David's current condition. We had to get him well enough for the transplant. And we needed to help him remain calm and assured: That was our primary objective; that was our plan. As hours passed, turning into days, and no root cause for the infection could be found, the plan seemed harder and harder to accomplish.

An infectious disease specialist joined Dr. Firstenberg and the MDA staff to work on David's case.

"We're 'troubleshooting'," Dr. F told us. "It's complicated. Because David has so many antibiotics in his body, it takes longer for the blood cultures to reveal anything."

Meanwhile, more tests and scans.

Many times I wanted to give in to fear. I wanted to let myself sink to the floor and sob until I had no breath, no tears left. I wanted to give up the effort to be strong, to say the positive words; I wanted to scream out the terror and frustration I felt until the rafters echoed with my pain. But always, before I could let myself collapse, I thought of David. Always, it was about David. I wanted to help him, to soothe him, to comfort and encourage him. What would my giving in accomplish? And haunting my heart was the fear that if I gave in, if I let myself begin to cry the deep, heart-sobs pulsing in my soul, would I ever be able to stop?

David was holding on to every thread of faith and hope. I couldn't let him see me let go. I didn't want to be a casualty in this battlefield of waiting. So, I made myself grab hold of the good news that a perfect donor was being readied for the transplant that would make David strong and healthy again. I imagined him just so: shooting baskets on *our* backyard court, hitting balls on the golf course. I made myself visualize him moving forward into a future of hope and joy. The vision carried me for a couple of days until I noticed he had begun to lose heart.

"I'm really tired of all these meds, mom," he said, his voice weak. "I don't like thinking about what they're doing to my body."

Once again, I wrapped myself in a façade of pleasant expressions and gentle gestures, and I spoke the words I thought he needed to hear. Words I desperately wanted to believe.

"It's okay, David," I murmured. "The drugs are going to get you well enough for the transplant. You've got to keep holding on to that good news. It's going to be fine."

The next day, a CT scan showed nodules in David's lungs. A pulmonologist joined his team of doctors. His illness continued to confound them all.

Tom began working less and spending most of his time at the hospital, with David and me. There was little reason to go home to sleep—sleep eluded us—but we tried anyway, waking often, and finally getting up and returning the hospital in the wee hours of the morning.

It was Thursday night, and David sent Tom to the Dairy Queen for a dipped cone. He was hungry, and that was a good sign. Ice cream tasted good to him. Tom stayed long after I went home, talking with his son, being alone with him. When he came home, he gathered the family and said, "Let's pray."

Andrew and Jon joined Tom and me, and we all knelt around our bed and cried out to God for answers. We begged God to reveal the cause of David's fever, the source of his infection. We begged God for healing.

It was a bittersweet time, without David among us. We talked, shared our thoughts, our fears. We wept, all of us; we spoke of our sadness. And each of us agreed that we felt a kind of release for having been together, prayed together, and cried together. Each of us was clinging to faith—that much was evident; and in that moment, each of us believed wholeheartedly that David would be healed.

The next day, now five days into testing, scans, more tests and more doctors assigned to David's case, we still had no answers. David's condition was worsening. The transplant date was coming at us quickly, and David was nowhere near ready. I had to fight the growing terror. I had to forbid myself to think about the possibility that he wouldn't be well enough to return to MD Anderson for the procedure.

David tried hard to be upbeat, but it became more difficult as his condition worsened. He found some small new bits of strength after a visit from Mary and Derek. They came at the perfect time. Tom and I slipped away for a quick meal at a nearby restaurant while David was dozing. He awoke to find his friends sitting in his room.

On Sunday morning, I awoke early, feeling the accustomed weight of worry and anxiety even before I opened my eyes. I got up and dressed quickly, choosing to do my worrying at David's bedside. I settled into the recliner in his room, nestling my limbs into the now-familiar dents in the cushions and studied my son's face. My thoughts whirled as I thought about the transplant.

If only we could get his blood counts to rise everything would improve from there.

If only the doctors could identify the infection…

Around 6:00 am, David woke up restless, coughing. I quickly moved to his side, speaking softly, touching him with cool fingers. His face was hot with fever.

"Today's going to be a better day," I said. "You're a fighter. You've been stubborn all your life, and you are not going to give up or give in."

David smiled.

"I know, there's no cancer growing in my body," he said.

"That's right. And the transplant donor is a perfect match, and he's willing to go through the procedure to help you. David, a total stranger is going to give you his stem cells! Can you believe it?"

"Yeah, cool, huh? Whoever he is, I hope he's an Aggie," Dave said. "Can't have Longhorn blood in my veins, that's for sure."

We both chuckled.

"Your friends at Kanakuk are praying for you. People everywhere are praying for you."

The mention of Kanakuk made David smile again. I knew he was thinking of Jennifer, missing her. The smile disappeared as a spasm of coughing convulsed him.

I gripped his hand and prayed, *Lord, heal his lungs, please... make his blood counts go up...please, Lord.*

Prayer was my lifeline. At every moment I was no more than a breath away from crying out to God.

Others were praying for us, for David; I knew that. But the truth was, at that time, I felt little consolation in that knowledge, even though I had used it to try to encourage David. I was seriously depleted, emotionally and physically. Both Tom and I were operating from a very small tank of reserves, and it was almost empty. We could do little more than put one foot in front of the other. Friends and family, Linda and Rick, Brenda and Tyler, were there for us without having to be asked, picking up the slack at home for us, helping with chores, meals, and in other ways I will probably never know. Even with their constant support, Tom and I were nearing total exhaustion and collapse.

I felt that sense of absolute emptiness as I sat next to David, listening to his breathing, cringing as he coughed. A couple of hours later, Tom joined me at the hospital. We watched a nurse help David out of bed and into the bathroom. His movements were slow, shaky; his body thin and tortured. Tom and I exchanged painful glances as we listened to the coughing and choking coming from behind the bathroom door.

When the nurse stepped out, we heard bits of a phone conversation and knew that a doctor was being summoned to David's room. Moments later, he was wheeled down the corridor to the Intensive Care Unit.

* * *

Tom's thoughts:

David's blood counts are not progressing as expected and needed. Normally, it takes three or four days after the end of the chemo treatment before the blood counts start to rebound. Could this be the reason why David is feeling "strange"? When we talked this afternoon, David said that it was "a different feeling this time." He said, "My stomach is bothering me." I'm looking at David and he seems fine to me. What could be occurring inside his body? Again, too many unanswered questions.

Somehow, our conversation shifts to an unbelievable topic: David tells me that he does not want his life to be extended through any type of life support. The tone of the conversation is very calm and matter of fact. I tell him, "You're not going to need any life support—that's not going to happen." But I understand his request.

David is six weeks away from his 21st birthday and we are talking about life support. I wonder what prompted this.

CHAPTER 17

Time sometimes does funny things. It seems to stand still when you want it to hurry; it rushes at you with ferocity when you need it to back up or stop altogether. In those moments when David was passing through the corridor toward the intensive care unit, I wanted time to stop. I wanted everything in the universe to stop. I wanted a space in the cosmos where clocks didn't tick, where time never ran out. I wanted to hide David in that space while the doctors figured out why he was so sick, while they readied him for the life-giving transplant. As a nurse moved alongside David's bed, rushing him through the hallways, I felt time speeding. I felt its utter disregard.

No time. No time to hug David before they hurried him away. No time to reassure him. No time for the comforting words we wanted to say. No time to wonder if I even believed the words anymore.

Today's going to be a better day... Had I whispered those words to David only minutes ago? Had he believed it?

His breathing rapid, shallow when he wakened, he was now coughing and spitting up blood, struggling just to catch his breath.

Today's going to be a better day... The words felt true when I spoke them, but now, shock and disbelief belied them.

"I've called a pulmonologist," a nurse told us as we followed David's bed to the ICU. "He'll wear an oxygen mask to help him breathe, and we'll be monitoring him more closely."

Tom and I nodded, sent David shaky smiles. I stepped aside to make three quick phone calls: to my sister Linda, my friend Brenda, and my pastor, Bruce Schmidt. Tom called Jon and Andrew. It was a familiar pattern: We mustered our family and friends to pray. All that was left was the waiting.

I was accustomed to sitting next to David's bed. I was accustomed to speaking to him, encouraging him. This time was no different. I continued with the mantra that we both had memorized.

"You'll be better soon, Dave. ...Hang in there with us..."

"...Your breathing is going to improve and we'll get you back to a regular room...You're going to be okay..."

The oxygen mask made it difficult for David to communicate, but we understood when he needed a sip of water or some ice chips. Occasionally he glanced at the TV where ESPN was playing. The voices of sportscasters droned softly in the background. Rick, Linda and Tyler came in for a few minutes. When Linda left, Rick and Tyler stayed, lingering in the room with us, standing quietly in the background as Andrew and Jon joined Tom and me around David's bedside.

Our conversations, soft and brief, revolved around sports, as usual. Andrew had a golf tournament the next day—a tournament David and Jon had played before. David knew the course well. At one point, he lifted his oxygen mask, grinned, and asked, weakly, "Do you think Andrew's going to hit 'em straight tomorrow at his tournament?"

Teasing followed, quiet reminiscences of golf balls in sand traps, triple bogies, and scores contested. David listened, eyes closed, occasionally nodding, grinning beneath his mask.

Late that night, Tom and the guys went home, and I curled up in an uncomfortable chair in the waiting area. Sleep eluded me, so I rose often to check on David, listen to his breaths, squeeze his hands. Except for the beeps and hums of monitors, the room was eerily quiet. David slept soundly, unaware of my presence, undisturbed by my occasional sobs.

Sometime that night, near the wee hours of the morning, David's nurse joined me at his bedside.

"You know, I feel like this is a ministry," she said, as she read the data on the monitors. "I see it as a calling, to care for my patients, and to pray for them. Sometimes when I'm with David I can feel the presence of angels everywhere."

I caught my breath.

"I don't feel it in every room, just in some. Right now I've got patients in two rooms where I feel the powerful comfort of angels."

I didn't know what to say, how to thank her. Speechless, I hugged her.

Were they there? The angels? Was the sense of warm comfort I felt in those moments the fanning of angel wings? I didn't know, but I welcomed the respite from cold terror that seemed to be hovering nearby.

The next morning, Tom met me at the hospital to take up the vigil with David, and I went home to sleep. I had not yet fallen into bed when Tom called to say he was sending Linda to bring me back to the hospital.

"Dr. Firstenberg wants to put David on a ventilator," Tom told me.

I couldn't comprehend what he was saying.

"David's heart is racing," Tom explained. "He needs to be lightly sedated to calm his heart. It will relax his body and help him breathe more easily."

My own heart began racing.

"We need to be with him now, before they put him into a light sleep, before he's on the ventilator. After, he won't be able to talk to us."

I caught the urgency in Tom's words and hurried to be ready when Linda arrived. I stepped into David's room, hoping I could once again find the strength needed to be the calming, soothing presence I wanted to be for David, for my family.

Soft words, gentle words passed between us in the next moments. David, too weak to reply, accepted our touches, our whispers, and smiled beneath his mask.

"David will make it," Tom and I told each other.

"He'll rebound and get the strength he needs to get the transplant," we said, reassuring each other."

I said, "He's got the strongest will of anyone I know."

Tom answered, "He's tenacious, for sure. People are praying, God's going to do a miracle."

Over and over we said these things to each other.

"He's going to get well and have an amazing testimony of faith that he'll be sharing with people when he's eighty-years-old," we told each other.

And we believed it.

Even though David lay in intensive care in a light, drug-induced sleep, we believed he could hear us. We believed that he would wake up and walk out one day, healed and strong, laughing and luminous with life. We stayed in that place of expectation, believing, because to do anything else felt like a betrayal of David, a betrayal of faith.

And so we continued our vigil. We continued our conversations.

"When Dave wakes up he's going to be so proud of the way Andrew played in that tournament."

"David is going to laugh so hard when he hears about..."

"David is going to be so surprised at all these kids who keep coming by the hospital....he's not going to believe who showed up this afternoon....I can't wait to tell him..."

If, somewhere in the deep recesses of my mind, there was a thought that David might not survive, I buried it even deeper and ran fast and far from any sign posts that might send me toward it.

David's treatment continued to be complicated. Several specialists worked with Dr. Firstenberg, troubleshooting, exploring, experimenting. Every medication brought another troubling consequence to David's body. As one drug caused damage to one part, another drug was administered, adjusted, bringing yet another consequence, another complication.

Tom and I spent most of the hours of every day at David's bedside. I never stopped taking notes, writing down questions I wanted to ask when the doctor made his rounds, jotting down the names of people who stopped by.

David will want to know who came to see him...he'll want to thank them all...

Every morning, when we arrived at the ICU, we found our friends Tyler and Rob sitting in the same chairs in the waiting area outside Dave's room. They arrived early before work every morning to pray and get a status report on Dave. But no one was present in the deep hours of the night to notice or say thank-you to Uncle Rick when he arrived to stand outside David's glass window to pray while Tom and I were home in fitful sleep.

One morning we saw Dr. Hampton, David's pediatrician, in the ICU hallway outside David's room.

"I was on call all night," he shrugged. "I just wanted to be here." He seemed reluctant to leave, as though he had more to say, but then he hurried out to make his rounds. Later that day he stopped by again.

"I didn't sleep much last night," he told us. "I talked to David some; I tried to share calming words with him. I memorized I Corinthians 13 a while back, and it all came back to me, just for David, I guess. I saw tears in the corners of his eyes while I was reciting the verses." Dr. Hampton choked back his own tears.

Such tenderness brought Tom and me to tears too.

David's friends never let us forget that they, too, were committed to standing with us and showing up for David. One morning, as Tom and I arrived at the ICU, we were startled to find David's friends in the waiting area. One was stretched out on the floor, two dozed in the awful chairs; one sipped coffee and whispered softly to another. All night they had hung out in that space, taking turns standing at the window by David's room, praying for him. One at a time—first Peter, then Micah, then Christopher, then Joseph, and then Brandon— they held vigil. Standing at the glass enclosure they could see only David's shadow through a curtain, but it was enough. They watched and prayed all night. When they weren't praying, they told funny stories about Dave and assured themselves that, somehow, David knew they were there, with him. They comforted themselves with the thought that he knew he was loved and prayed for.

I hoped they were right. I hoped David knew we were all there for him, with him, that we would not stop praying.

Before they left, Tom arranged with the head nurse to let the guys go into David's room, if only for three or four minutes. They stood a few steps away from his bed and bowed their heads as Tom prayed that David would know that his friends were there; that he would know that we all still believed in the miracle of healing.

"We're not giving up," the boys said.

Tom and I walked out with them and watched them disappear down the hallway. I wrapped my arms around myself, holding closely their sweet gestures of love, praying these would help me return to David's bedside with hope.

Later that afternoon, a doctor arrived with good news: David's body was still clear of cancer cells; the white blood cell count had increased a bit; his chest x-ray looked slightly better, and he was requiring less oxygen through the ventilator.

"It's steady improvement," the doctor said. "We'll keep fine-tuning our plan for his treatment."

And we'll keep praying for a miracle, I added silently.

I bent to drop a kiss on David's forehead, and then Tom and I went out to deliver the good news to the dear friends who had come to spend the day near us. Several friends were there waiting for the latest word.

Tom stood among us all, lowered his head, and then began to speak.

"When I was with David, I felt the Holy Spirit impress on me that we are to pray for a miracle of healing for David. I strongly sensed God telling me that David will be healed and walking out of this hospital in seven days. If God can create heaven and earth in seven days, he can heal our son in seven days."

Seven days. That would be Thursday, June 16th. In a sudden surge of faith, I could see my son, well and healed, standing, walking out of the hospital.

Tears flowed among us all in that moment. Together, we claimed the words God spoke to Tom, and together we let ourselves ride a wave of hope and exultation. Not one among us doubted God could do this mighty thing. Our pastor, Bruce, and his wife Martha, stood with us in our circle, holding our hands, sharing our emotions. We felt comfort and reassurance as Bruce read scripture and prayed that God would work through our special team of physicians and accomplish this miracle for David.

By Saturday, June 11, David's team of specialists had grown to include a urologist, an infectious disease specialist, a gastroenterologist and a vascular surgeon. Dr. Su, the pulmonologist already on board, told us that while both lungs appeared to be improving, David had to keep getting better. There was no room for regression.

David was desperately ill. So ill, in fact, that Dr. Su labeled him the sickest patient in the entire hospital at that time. When he spoke those words to Tom and me, I felt crushed.

My son—my dear David—was the sickest patient in the hospital.

I couldn't make sense of it. Yes, I knew his condition was grave. Yes, I knew that his body was traumatized. But I had formed a small, guarded sanctuary of hope in my heart, and the doctor's words were an unwelcome intrusion.

* * *

Tom's reflections, June 12th:

The strain of David's presence in ICU is wearing on me. However, I am fortunate to spend every day with David and not worry about anything else. My partners and associates at the accounting firm are covering my absence day after day. I feel most comfortable sitting with David in his ICU room and stepping out once in a while to visit with people in the waiting room.

The hardest part is the beginning of each day. In the mornings before I leave for the hospital, I feel the Holy Spirit interceding on my behalf in my weakness, because I cannot effectively pray. Romans 8:28 is a special part of the Bible, but for me, Romans 8:26 is a true testimony of God's provision to me. "In the same way, the Spirit helps us in our weakness. We do not know what we ought to pray for, but the Spirit himself intercedes for us with groans that words cannot express." I literally groan in my inability to pray for David each morning, yet the Holy Spirit intercedes every day on my behalf.

Each morning in the waiting room of the ICU, I see Rob and Tyler already there praying for David. Their presence is another provision from God. It is comforting to see how God uses others to minister to someone who is hurting. We speak briefly and then I walk from the waiting area to David's room. The walk has almost become an overbearing event as I will soon know whether David's condition has improved or not. Lately, no improvement has occurred.

Through the anxiety and the waiting, I truly believe that David will soon be better.

* * *

Tom was hopeful. He was full of faith, even when he was most sad. I leaned on him, depending on his hope when mine was weak.

Everyday, we sensed God's strength. If we had energy and emotion, it was because God poured it into us, and we shared whatever we had with each other. And we drew on the strength of our friends—strength God gave them to bring to us when they showed up at the ICU and camped out in the waiting area. We absorbed comfort from notes and phone messages and words sent to us from people who were aware of our dire circumstances.

One day, Nancy, the mother of Jon's girlfriend, called and left this message: "Laura, I just wanted you to know that the Holy Spirit wakes me up many times every night to prompt me to pray for David. I've been up many hours most nights, praying for David and for your family."

Stories like this came to us often, sometimes several a day. Many mentioned June 16th, the day we were expecting to see David whole and well, walking out the hospital doors. But that day was coming at us quickly. Things needed to start turning around fast.

Tuesday, June 14th, Tom and I arrived at David's room to learn of Dr. F's request to more heavily sedate him. We consented; we had no choice.

We sat close to him, speaking to him, believing that he could hear us. We named the friends who had stopped by, the ones lounging in the waiting area, the ones who had called and sent him letters and emails. All the while, machinery hummed and tubes flowed, doors swung open and closed as nurses and technicians came and went. Tom and I ignored everything but David. I caressed his hand, told stories, and prayed until the heaviness became too much.

"It's okay if we leave for an hour or so," Tom said. "Jon and Andrew will be here in a little while. Let's go home, we need to think."

It was true. We needed to think. We needed time away from the hospital sounds in order to hear our own hearts.

At home, Tom left to take a walk. I puttered for a few minutes and then, exhausted, I dropped into a chair to pray and be still. In my stillness, more and more thoughts entered my mind, each clearer than the one before. Suddenly, I needed Tom to come home.

I heard the back door open and the sound of footsteps, and then silence. I waited. I went to the kitchen to find Tom.

"Are you all right?" I asked.

His head bowed, his shoulders slumped, he looked as beaten down as I felt.

"I have something important to tell you," I said, leading him toward a chair.

"And I have something to tell you." Tom stammered. "I was walking and I felt like God was telling me that David is not going to survive. I strongly feel that I was just told I need to prepare the eulogy for David's service—soon."

"That's what I was going to tell you," I said. "I think God said David's isn't going to get well."

The message was like a sword in my heart, but I had to share it with Tom. The speaking of it, sharing it, hearing it from each other seemed to validate it, prove its truth, but the pain of it was beyond words.

In those moments, Tom and I both knew: David was going to heaven soon.

My chest heaved, ached with the sobs. Through tears, I spoke, "Honey, we need to go to David and release him back to the Lord. He was *His* child first, before he belonged to us. I feel like God has revealed to me that it is time. He was a gift to us, on loan for 21 years, and I believe David is waiting on us."

I spoke the words and heard the truth resonate in my spirit.

"David sees what is waiting for him in Glory. He needs us to tell him he's free—free to go be with Jesus. He needs us to tell him we will be all right and he's free!"

Tom wrapped his arms around me and we held each other, our sobs rocking us in the rhythm of unimaginable grief.

Sorrow so deep, so profound, sent us to an island totally disconnected from the rest of the world. It was a surreal place, inhabited by no one but ourselves, just Tom and me. We were alone there. Alone with each other, and yearning for the felt presence of our God. We drove to our church, joined hands, and knelt in the beautiful sanctuary where David had worshipped with us, the place where he had shared with the congregation the story of his cancer and the miracle of remission just six months earlier.

"I'm excited to stand before you—not to brag about *my* strength and courage, but to brag about my *God*."

David's words seemed to echo off the walls of the sanctuary. He had been so strong, so sure, so beautiful in his faith.

How I needed that faith, that strength and certainty now, in this moment.

Yet, had God not given both Tom and me a clear message, simultaneously? Could He not equip us with courage and wisdom? Could He not enable us to release our child to Him?

We were still on our knees, crying out to God, when three staff pastors joined us. They pulled us into their arms and began praying with us, for us. Enveloped in their love, I felt the power of the Holy Spirit as all our heartache and grief and fear spilled out before God. Sometime later we stood up on trembling limbs, weak and exhausted, knowing David waited for us at Arlington Memorial Hospital, just a short drive from the church.

Feeling sick, our hearts aching, we entered David's room. When the nurse left, we stood on either side of David's bed. We leaned down, hovering close to his face. In those moments, I didn't hear the familiar noise of the ventilator or the monitors' beeping. Nothing and no one existed for me except my son. His thin, lanky body lay under the sheets, sleeping quietly. I was drawn to his hands; his large left hand lay in front of me and appeared so strong and healthy. As I touched and caressed his hand, Tom rubbed his head, soft with the growth of new hair now that chemotherapy no longer poisoned his body.

"We were so close, David, so close to your transplant..." I murmured.

I thought of our lives without him in the years to come—many years, so many years. Without David. The pain of it was literal, sharp; it stole my breath.

How will we ever get through this?

I gripped his hand firmly, holding on as if I could keep him with me. That used to work—holding David's hand. When he was small I could grasp it quickly when we were in a crowd or crossing a street. I could keep him safe, keep him with me. A swell of fresh pain nearly drowned me as I remembered how he had resisted my pull. He never liked to slow down. He never liked to be held back.

Large hands, they had grown to the perfect size for dribbling a basketball and shooting three pointers on the court; they were perfect for gripping a golf club and sending the ball soaring long and straight down the fairway.

Perfect hands for strumming a guitar—he was teaching himself to play Uncle Rick's when he got sick.

He could build anything with Legos when he was a child. His creation of a pirate ship and its entourage was something to see! We used to say we should have bought stock in the Lego® company.

Tom's voice broke through my memories.

"We were so close, David...so close."

Through the din of our sobs, I heard him pray, asking God for strength. There was more to say. We weren't through speaking to David, but our throats ached and our tears choked us.

We lingered. We whispered the words we so desperately needed to speak to David. We tried to gather ourselves, breathe and pray, before Jon and Andrew joined us with David. Together, we cried and spoke and touched David's hands and face. Together we gave him our love, and we relinquished our precious son into God's hands.

"He's hearing every word," I said to Tom and the boys. "I believe that with all my heart," I whispered, leaning close to him, letting my tears fall on his cheeks. "He knows we're here, he hears us; he knows we love him."

The next hours passed as had many nights in the ICU—nurses in and out, Tom and I stirring to check on David, to check on each other, finally going home to sleep. Our exhaustion was beyond describing, yet we hated leaving David's side. When the morning dawned, on Wednesday, June 15th, we returned to David's side with aching hearts and bodies.

When Dr. Firstenberg stepped into Dave's room, earlier than usual, he surprised us with a glimmer of hope.

"There is one last option we can try," he said. "We can administer one more transfusion to try to kick-start his blood counts to get them to start producing. It's a rare injection of white blood cells."

If there was anything that might help David, we were willing to try. If his blood count began to rise, the bone marrow transplant could still be viable at the end of the month.

Late that evening, in our home, Tom and I gathered with Jon and Andrew to pray for this last effort for David. This one small thread of hope was enough to keep us holding on. We couldn't give up yet.

The morning of June 16th resembled any other morning. We drove to the hospital parking garage and rode the elevator to the third floor. Tom and I rushed past the waiting area. Without stopping to chat, we briefly acknowledged Rob and Tyler sitting together in their usual places, as well as Linda and Rick. We hurried into David's room, and moments later Dr. F arrived with good news.

"The blood for the transfusion arrived. We're ready," Doctor F told us.

It seemed every moving part had finally landed in place. The transfusion to jump-start Dave's blood counts could proceed. Tom and I drew deep breaths and nodded to each other, to the doctor. We were impatient, uncertain. Our hopes had been crushed so many times, we were afraid to be optimistic, but not ready to give up. Dr. F had called this transfusion our "last option." We were given little hope but had nothing to lose.

Dave lay so still, so silent. I watched as Dr. F moved around his bed, checking him, studying the readings on the equipment, as he always did. His movements deliberate, he leaned over to shine a light into David's eyes. He lingered, stood, bent to look again, and then turned to Tom and me.

"I need to call the neurologist," he said.

I felt startled, confused.

"One of his eyes is dilated, one is not. This is a sign of a possible brain hemorrhage."

The words hung in the air, dark, impenetrable. I couldn't understand.

"Tom..." I turned to my husband.

His arms circled me, held me, as the truth of the doctor's words settled upon me.

I remember the flurry of activity as doctors and nurses surrounded David's bed. Hushed voices spoke while I stood silent, stunned, numbed. Gentle arms guided me out of the room, directing me down the hall into a private room where Tom and I were joined by Linda and Rick. Moments later a neurologist entered and gave us the grim news.

"It appears that several blood clots shot to David's brain," he told us. "He suffered a massive stroke this morning. Both sides of his brain are affected."

I heard the words but I couldn't make sense of them.

It was June 16th. This was the day we wanted to believe David would leave the hospital. This was the day David was supposed to go home with us, the day Tom felt compelled to pray for his healing.

In my imagination I had played this day—the day of his healing—over and over. I had seen my tall, lanky son, stand and walk out. Too thin—he had been so sick—but alive and ready to take his life back: that was how I had envisioned it. The setbacks had been many, and I had prayed for courage to release him to God, if that was God's plan; I felt I *had* released him. But then hope came again—small, fragile—but hope, nonetheless. I was not prepared for its utter demise.

I was not prepared for the truth that was being laid out for me, for all of us.

The letting go—it wasn't supposed to be like this: the unplugging of a machine, the slow wait for his heart to stop beating.

We could choose when; we could wait as long as we needed, to be ready, to be sure. We would need to tell Jon and Andrew as soon as they arrived at the hospital. After the extended family had a chance to say their goodbyes, then the four of us would enter into David's ICU room for the last time.

Who is ever ready? Who can ever be sure?

It was 10:00 a.m. We knew what we must do. We would gather around David, as a family; we would pray and talk to him, share stories, I would caress his hands. All the while, I would wonder if he could hear, if he knew the depths of love we felt for him, the depths of joy he had brought into our lives.

In the midst of my grief, my thoughts turned often to Jon and Andrew. I ached for Andrew's pain and confusion—he was only seventeen. I prayed for him, as I prayed for David. And I prayed for Jon whose younger brother, closest to him in age, lay dying. All three were so close.

The hours passed. When the afternoon arrived, we knew it was time.

We would let him go.

We stood together. The machine unplugged, silence settled.

For more than an hour David's heart refused to quit. It was strong—it had always been strong, like a lion.

Everything about David had been strong. His will, his humor, his passion, his faith.

I tried to be strong too, David, for you. And then, *I don't have to be strong anymore.*

It was over.

It was June 16th, and David was home. It was God's perfect will and timing. David was healed.

CHAPTER 18

Tom's reflections, June 18, 2005

Tonight I am writing my son's eulogy. I feel God has been preparing me to do this, but I don't really understand, and I feel great conflict. I want my words to tell about a young man whose life was full of fun, excitement and action—a life of faith. But where do I begin? How do I start?

Memories and emotions are whipping through my mind at warp speed. How do I capture them and shape them and record them? I keep returning to the memory of David's birth—how Laura and I rushed through the heart of Arlington at 1:00 in the morning. I drove 70 miles an hour through the city streets, hoping to get to the hospital before David arrived. He came into the world with personality and spunk that stayed with him. But I have to start even further back than that.

Laura and I are convinced David was conceived at Disney World. We took a short trip, just to get away for a few days. The night David was conceived, we rode the biggest rollercoaster at the park. We have always believed that set the tone for the kind of life David would live—a rollercoaster life of fun and thrills. I'm not sure how that story will go over at his memorial service, but I think people will understand, if they knew David at all. Maybe it will set the tone for the service—I want it to be uplifting, positive, even joyful. Because that is how I want David to be remembered. He loved to laugh. He lived as though life itself was a celebration.

I loved being a father to David, as I did with Jon and Andrew. I loved the time we spent together, playing sports—almost any sport with a ball in it. I loved teaching David life lessons and watching him grow and mature.

I remember his junior high days—chaperoning him at school dances. I remember seeing another dad shine a flashlight between David and his dance partner, insisting that they create some space between each other.

I remember how he grew eight inches during the fall of his sophomore year in high school, and how he loved playing basketball and golf.

I remember his first speeding ticket. So many firsts: his first golf tournament, his first win. I remember all the hours he spent preparing for the Mr. Viking contest and for the UIL competition in accounting in Austin. It was all happening over a two week period during his senior year—it was non-stop—but that was David. He was always in motion, and we were always trying to keep up with him.

Joining Jon at Texas A&M was a dream come true for David. I felt great satisfaction as I watched him fully immerse himself into college life. No one ever loved college, or Texas A&M, more than David did.

I remember David's fight with cancer.

It is difficult now, thinking about those painful days. But I don't want this to be a sad eulogy. David wasn't sad. He was joyful and lively. I want to honor that about him.

As I write, I wonder, am I boasting?

Is it okay to be proud of David and the life he lived?

There is no doubt that the centerpiece of David's life was his relationship with Jesus Christ. I want to close the eulogy with this part of his life—that which was most important to him. I think I can do it without breaking down.

Again, memories are precious.

I remember how Laura and I watched David's faith mature during his junior year of high school; how that maturation kept moving forward while he was at A&M, how it began to intertwine with all the parts of his life. It is that maturity and the knowledge of the strength of his faith that will sustain us during this grieving process.

David relied on God during his battle with cancer. That reliance inspired his family and many others.

Tonight, I can't stop thinking about heaven. My family will reconnect there, and we will live together through eternity. I feel comfort, somehow.

I have read over what I've written—the thoughts and memories that will compose a eulogy for my son David. I pray this will be a confirmation of a significant life. I hope I've done a good job.

CHAPTER 19

To hold a pen and write words—I watched my husband record the memories of family life with David. My own pen lay still, untouched. I couldn't write. The journal I had so carefully written in for the past year was closed. My body moved as though programmed to do the most basic tasks, nothing more. Yet there was much to be done, scores of decisions to be made—decisions no parent ever imagines having to make.

We now inhabited the reality we had tried to outrun for most of the past year. Our child had died; we had to bury him. And then we had to figure out how to go on living. Tom and I were concerned about Jon and Andrew. How would they deal with their loss?

Everything felt impossible, overwhelming. Weakened, disoriented, I could not navigate the many details. It helped that Linda and Rick drove us to the funeral home and sat with us as the staff counselor offered us options for a casket, the burial plot (we chose a place near the pond—David loved water so much), the obituary details. At times I felt a sense of the ludicrous, the implausible—this couldn't really be happening—then the chaos of grief would swamp me, and I felt numb and afraid.

Human feelings, all of them, but they felt new to me—as though I was feeling them for the first time. I wondered who I was, this mother, whose son had died. Who would I be now, after? Everything felt different. In that private, maternal place in my soul, I dwelled on the memories. I recalled the brave "letting go" moments with the children. I remembered letting them go to kindergarten on the frightening first day, then the first day as each entered middle school, and then the powerful "letting go" moments as we watched each son drive away at age 16 with a new driver's license. I thought those were hard, and they were. But nothing can prepare a mom and dad to let go of a son or daughter and say goodbye in this earthly world—leaving us behind, letting them go ahead of us. It caused such chaos in my mind—I couldn't grasp even a thread of the finality of it all.

My life, my home felt unfamiliar to me. People came and went, bringing food and drinks. One arrived with a supply of toilet paper and Kleenex. I felt relief—I didn't have to concern myself with such things. At that moment I was preoccupied with gathering all the special photos of David to use for a DVD during his service. An avalanche of memories buried me, making the emotional task of sifting through family pictures even more difficult, more painful.

The visitation was scheduled for Sunday evening, June 19th, 6:00-8:00 p.m. I felt great sadness when I realized that it was Father's Day. How would Tom endure it? How would any of us endure?

Prayer. We needed prayer. Those who had prayed for us so faithfully for the past months must continue to pray, or our hearts would not be able to survive the pain of it all. I grabbed hold of the certainty that my friends would keep praying—they had to. I knew they wouldn't stop now, in this hour of our greatest grief.

The night arrived, hot and humid. People stood in line for three hours, waiting their turn to hug Tom, the boys, and me, shake our hands, and assure us of their love and continuing prayers. I remember the crush of people, the hum of conversations, and a supernatural sense of being held up, supported, able to stand and not break although standing in the path of a great storm of sadness. I remember a friend handing me sips of ice cold water throughout the evening. I remember being aware of kind words, feeling them, more than hearing them, and thanking God for them.

I felt oddly comforted by the crowd. It was strong evidence that our family was not alone in our grief, nor were we alone in our love for David. People had driven to Arlington for miles, for hours, to be here with us and to honor David. One in particular triggered a fresh flow of tears. When Jeannie Barrett, David's accounting teacher, introduced herself, I couldn't contain my emotions. She drove three hours from College Station, knowing she wouldn't be able to stay for the memorial service the next morning, but not wanting to miss the chance to say good-bye to David.

"I needed to be here," she told me.

Many others echoed her words.

It was a night of searing pain. Shaken, numb, our family was still in shock, feeling as though we were lost, wandering in a surreal painting. Nothing was as it should be. And yet, somehow, messages of comfort found their way into our souls.

The following morning, the funeral home sent a driver and a limo to our home, only to discover that we, disoriented in our grief, had forgotten he was coming. He sat in front of our house, waiting, wondering, for several minutes, before learning that we had driven ourselves to the church.

Every funeral has common elements: the silence, the mild scent of flowers, the bowed heads of friends and relatives. This funeral was uncommon in every way: this was my son's funeral—a funeral I never expected to attend. The scent of flowers was strong, filling every niche of the large sanctuary. The hush of the crowd was barely contained, as though tears or laughter could erupt at any moment. Young people, college students, stood together with parents, grandparents, professors, neighbors. It was a gathering of multiple generations of people who had known David. Their heads up, their faces forward, they came to share our grief and celebrate with us the life of David.

I listened as one by one David's closest friends and his cousin Laura walked to the podium to tell stories of his antics, his love of sports, his faith, his sense of humor, his kindness. I laughed. I cried. I leaned close to Tom, feeling the comfort of his shoulder, hoping he could feel something of the same from me.

When Dave's friend and mentor Cliff spoke, he said, "I'm going to ask you to stand if your life was truly impacted by the life of David Gilbert."

I heard a rustling behind me.

Then Cliff said, "Tom, Laura, Jon and Andrew, I'd like you to stand and turn around and see the impact of David's life."

Standing to face us were 1500 people—smiling, wiping tears, nodding. I felt my breath catch. Stunned, amazed, overwhelmed, I felt a flood of love for all of them, and I felt their love flowing back to me, toward Tom and the boys. We were not alone in our love for David; we were not alone in our sorrow. A sense of joyful celebration mingled with the deep pain of loss.

The celebration continued as Jon took the podium to tell a special story of David. He told about Daisy's visit to David's room at MD Anderson.

"Daisy read Psalm 91 with Mom and David that night," Jon said. He reminded us of the truth of the words.

He is my refuge and fortress...
His faithfulness is a shield and rampart."

I remembered the comfort I felt that night in the hospital—David receiving chemo, Daisy so kind and comforting. I remember knowing that God had sent her, as surely as He sent the sunset that evening. I remember knowing He was present; He was faithful.

Now, months later, sitting in my church, surrounded by the scent of funeral bouquets, I watched my husband step up to deliver our son's eulogy. I begged God for new assurance of that faithfulness, for me, for Tom, for all of us.

When Tom returned to my side, Pastor Bruce made closing remarks. The music played. David's special friends, pall bearers, walked out of the church with us. As I walked, I kept hearing his friend Peter's words, "David's name was appropriate—he was a man after God's own heart."

Somehow, comfort found me and carried me through to the grave site.

I remember little of those moments, other than overwhelming sorrow. I remember going home, without David, and thinking how empty the house was, even though friends followed us home. I remember discovering the freezer filled with food, the table laden with sandwiches, fruit, desserts. I remember wondering what I would do when everyone left, yet knowing instinctively that my family would need the quietness and solitude. We would stumble around in the darkness of grief in a quest for relief, for peace.

Would we find it?

I wondered. And I wept.

*　*　*

Tom's reflections, June 20, 2005

Today I buried my son. I will never spend another earthly moment with him. Tonight, I sense loneliness and sadness that I fear will be a constant companion for a long time. Back home now, we talk among ourselves, but I can't concentrate on anything. I am depleted, numb. I have no idea what is in store tomorrow. Only five days ago we circled David's bed in ICU and said our good-byes to him. We planned a funeral service. Visitation was on Sunday, the memorial service today. I remember seeing people throughout the five days, somehow interacting with them, not breaking down. It is like I am in a light daze, able to function but not feeling anything. I remember holding Laura's hand during the service. After the service, I received condolences from close friends in the church foyer; some were crying and hugging me. I couldn't respond other than to nod and smile. At the grave site, more friends and family, then back to the church to eat with them all. Who can eat? I don't remember much else, except posing for a picture of three generations of Gilbert men—my father, myself, and my sons. David is missing.

CHAPTER 20

In the days after David's funeral and burial, I learned that layers of shock and numbness peel away slowly, ungently, exposing the heart, leaving it raw and throbbing. I found myself yearning for that numbness, for the sense of shock I felt at his graveside that had insulated me from the full onslaught of the reality of his death. But every day seemed to force the truth deeper into my soul.

My son had died.

I felt awkward, moving back and forth between realization and disbelief, always knowing I was traveling toward the excruciating reality. There was no turning back, only the inevitable arrival at the truth of life without my second son.

After all our prayers, all our faith and trust in the healing nature of the Almighty God, David had died. God didn't heal him—not the way we asked, not the way we needed him to be healed. Hard questions pounded my heart. No easy answers came.

I knew that my God was a very personal God. I believed He understood my every emotion. My need for Him was greater than it had ever been. With desperate yearning, I begged for a sense of intimacy with Him, for comfort, for help. I knew I couldn't travel this grief journey without Him. My journey would be unlike Tom's, unlike Jon's and Andrew's. Each of us would have to move through this unfamiliar place in our own unique way, without comparisons, without judgments.

We would have to learn to allow each other space to mourn; our family would have to learn to come together for comfort, sharing the common threads that bound us to David, to each other. Those moments of connection, when we shared memories—both the happy ones and the sad ones—these became precious to me. Chuckling softly, sometimes laughing out loud at some remembered antic of David's—these shared moments eased our pain, kept us feeling like a family. We recounted conversations with David, reminding each other of his comical ways, his love of life, his enjoyment of people. These things served as an underground current of energy for me, prompting me to keep breathing through the pain, keep moving my limbs, enabling me to perform the mundane tasks associated with life.

David's 21st birthday arrived exactly one month to the day after his passing. July 16th—it was a heartbreaking time for us. The idea he didn't live to see his 21st birthday was still unfathomable to us. But in the middle of our confusion and sorrow, a celebration began to take shape exceeding anything our weary minds could have planned. One by one, David's friends began showing up at our house. As his girlfriend Jenn and his mentor Cliff arrived, along with several other close friends, the day unfolded like the unwrapping of a gift.

I was surrounded by Tom, Andrew, Jon and Stephanie, as well as others who had dearly loved David. Rick, Linda and family, as well as Tyler, Brenda and their family, came over. Our home was full, bursting with people who were determined we would not be alone to mourn our son on his 21st birthday. Two close friends from our neighborhood generously opened their homes, offering guest rooms to David's friends when they learned the kids had planned a 24-hour celebration. They would be attending church with us the next morning.

As David would have wanted, I made his favorite Tex-mex meal: Chimichangas, with all the works. The noise and movement of friends and family in the kitchen, spilling out into various rooms in the house, was like sweet music. It seemed to exorcise the haunting gloom that had begun to feel familiar.

The plan was to caravan to the cemetery and continue the celebration of David's birthday there. I felt dread creeping into my heart. The sweet music of only moments before seemed elusive to me; I felt frightened, overwhelmed. I wanted to be able to reach back into my kitchen where laughter and jovial conversations had swirled around food and funny memories. I wanted to wrap myself in the noise, like an armor, to protect from the silence of the grave.

Oh, God. Help me....help me...

One by one, each vehicle rolled into the cemetery and parked near the grave site. I steeled myself for the moment when I would once again have to face the reality that David was gone.

Buried.

As I climbed out of the car, I saw Cliff pointing to the sky and everyone began looking up. There, arcing in the July sky, I saw a rainbow. Not a rain cloud was in sight, but there was the most beautiful rainbow I had ever seen gracing our Texas sky. I stood still, silent, letting the beauty of it spill over me. For just a moment, I felt pure joy, pure peace, and gratitude.

This is for you, Laura... It was God's voice in my heart *You're going to be all right...*

The message was clear—as clear as the colors of the rainbow. I felt hope. I felt courage.

I felt loved.

I approached the grave site, blinking tears, but feeling peaceful, unafraid.

Tom had made arrangements for a canopy to be set up over David's grave so that we could have some relief from the Texas sun while we shared birthday cake and celebrated his life. On the grassy area surrounding his grave, we set out blankets, older folks opened lawn chairs, everyone shared stories about David—some were ridiculously funny. There we were laughing, wiping tears, holding hands, sometimes hugging.

This is what David would have wanted, I thought. *His spirit is with us—I can feel it...* And then suddenly it occurred to me, *He probably instigated this whole thing!*

It was, after all, his 21st birthday.

At one point, another car pulled up, parked, and a tall, thin, bearded fellow climbed out. He approached Tom and me. It was Bart, another of David's good friends from A&M. Tom and I were thrilled to see him.

"I'm just off my flight from Italy. Nic sends his best wishes as well, but he's heading to Houston," Bart continued. "We hated to miss David's final days. I had to come by, pay my respects." He hugged Tom and me.

I remembered Bart and Nic were studying abroad. David had been so excited for them. Now Bart was home, standing at the grave of his friend, sharing our sorrow. One more friend who had made such great effort to honor David—once again I was struck with the poignancy of searing pain and sweet gratitude—such an unlikely mix in the human soul—and a surge of joy, as well.

Had it been only four weeks? Four weeks since we buried David?

I stood at his grave, among loving friends and family, filled with wonder at the peace I felt. Peace, and joy, mingling with the pain. I wondered if the peace and joy would linger after loving friends went home. I wondered if such a celebration would ever happen again.

I wondered if he would be forgotten. Would his friends note his birthday in future years?

Would they remember his laugh, his lanky stride? Would they want to return here and spend time recalling David and his life?

I pushed aside the questions and focused on being as close to David as I could. That was what we all wanted that day. And we did feel his presence. We felt it in the telling of stories and in the laughter of shared memories. I mused with curiosity as I watched Megan and Jay console and entertain one another – two of David's special friends who had just met at his memorial service. They were a good match, I thought, sensing a nod of David's approval.

At sunset Tom unloaded the golf bag from the car and, one by one, we took turns hitting golf balls over—or into—the pond. It was now a tradition, begun on the evening of David's burial, and now shared again on the anniversary of his birth. As a celebration of his life by the people who knew and loved him best, we each took a swing at a golf ball, and we each imagined David's face, alight with his mischievous grin.

The weekend over, friends and family departed, and once again I was left with the harsh reality of David's death. As the next weeks passed, my pain increased. I had no choice but to confront the reality that David was gone. The permanent marker placed at his grave three months later was, even in its beauty, a cruel reminder of death's finality: Son, Brother, Friend, Aggie, God's Child. Beneath those words, the Bible reference, Galatians 2:20.

Standing there, I tried to connect with the words that had such meaning for David:

"I have been crucified with Christ; it is no longer I who live,
but Christ lives in me; and the life which I now live in the flesh
I live by faith in the Son of God, who loved me and gave Himself for
me."

It was true: David no longer lived in the flesh, but he was alive
and living with the Son of God whom he loved. Yet, the words dug
deep furrows of pain in my soul. I wished for the peace I had felt in
this place only weeks earlier, on his birthday, surrounded by his
friends. But peace was gone. Only pain remained. Standing there,
looking down at the beauty of the headstone, I couldn't envision a
time when I would ever be without this searing heartache.

We were a family in pain, each of us confused, hurting. I worried
about us. Would we ever recover a sense of family life without
David? Would we ever be able to move beyond this place of grief
that seemed to be sapping us all of joy? What would our family feel
like?

I was one woman among three men. I had always been the one to
prompt communication. I was the "talker", the instigator of
conversations about feelings, emotions. Now, stuck in my own pain,
I felt inadequate, unable to help these three whom I loved more than
my own life. I watched them fearfully. What in their lives had ever
tutored them in the art of grieving well? Would they come out of this
with their souls intact?

Tom and I shared with each other our low, depressed spirits. Jon
felt the weight of grief but was comforted by the love of Stephanie in
his life. It was Andrew I most feared for. Andrew, throughout the
past year, had been in the trenches with us, fighting for David's life,
while his friends were enjoying their most memorable high school
experiences. Now, Andrew, only 17, was grieving heavily. He was
driving to the cemetery many evenings, hanging out at David's
grave, while those same friends were indulging in the summer fun
and freedom vouchsafed only for teenagers.

It was time for us to get help.

"You have to take one day at a time," the counselor told us. "You
can't rush the grief process. You won't ever be able to rush back into
life as it was."

He looked around the room at us, together for this first family session, and he warned us, "You'll have days where you'll be in nothing more than survivor mode."

I knew that mode —I felt as though I spent most of my time there.

I looked at Jon and Tom and Andrew. My heart broke for their pain as well as my own.

I listened as the counselor asked the right questions, triggering memories, giving release to emotions in my husband and my sons. They seemed to be able to accept the counselor; they seemed to be connecting with him, feeling at ease. He shared their love of golf and all things athletic. He welcomed our stories about family vacations and shared memories. He soon had Jon and Andrew talking about the things they would miss most about David. They recounted stories, at times, laughing together. As a mother, my own pain was doubled by the weight of theirs. I was thankful that here, in this place, at least, they were each willing to share their struggles and their feelings. Here, maybe each of us could get the help we needed to learn how to live without David.

A second session continued to help us articulate our hearts, give voice to our sadness, and share our grief as a family. I was surprised when, at the end of the time, the counselor told us, "You're doing all the right things." He explained, "As a family, you are dealing with incredible heartache, and you are doing as well I think it's possible, given your loss. Keep doing what you're doing."

I was surprised. I thought, Okay, but can we do it? Can we keep talking to each other, and listening, sharing our memories? Can we keep giving each other space to feel our pain and grieve in our own unique ways? Can we heal?

Tom was confident. He was sure we could still have meaningful talks, as a family, without a counselor involved. But as the days, weeks passed, it became clear that Tom and I were blindly grappling with our emotions—often his were very different from mine. Communicating with each other, trying to identify our feelings for each other —it was exhausting beyond words. We needed more help. "Grief Share", a ministry at our church, was the place where we found it. Listening to others share their experiences with grief planted seeds of hope in our hearts. We heard many stories about grieving the loss of a child, and we learned to recognize emotions that were indicators of some movement toward recovery. At the same time, it became clear to us that we were dramatically changed people. We would never again be who we were only a few short weeks ago.

Our lives had changed. Our marriage had changed. We weren't used to having to work so hard to understand, to be understood, to stay connected to each other. Grief exhausted us. We had been told the statistic: 80% of marriages eventually end in divorce after the death of a child. We were determined not to let that happen to us. By God's grace, we would work as hard as it took to love each other well while we mourned the death of our son. We would not let our grief separate us.

Early in our grieving we discovered that when one of us was deeply depressed, the other was feeling a bit stronger, able to do the heavy lifting from the bottom of the pit. We seemed to take turns, first one, and then the other, as though spelling each other. We vowed to be intentional about our concern for each other, about being connected and caring. It was hard work, but we weren't willing to give up on the relationship in which we had already invested over 27 years.

The night of September 6, 2005, was a night I will never forget. Tom, Andrew, Jon and Stephanie, and I found ourselves at A&M, engulfed by approximately 20,000 Texas Aggies, participating in the Silver Taps—a tradition created to honor members of the Aggie family who have died.

The A&M motto says "When an Aggie falls, the family comes together to remember." Every year, on April 21st, the Aggie Muster is held to honor any current and former student who has died the previous year. Silver Taps is held monthly as a special tribute to current students who have died. For more than 100 years, Aggies have observed these two traditions, coming together to honor and remember the passing of their classmates and friends. It was one of the things David most loved about Texas A&M. He loved the idea of customs and long-standing ceremonies; he loved being a part of a community of men and women who honored the traditions of the past; a community who valued the contribution of every Aggie, from every generation. He loved the "Aggie Spirit." I knew he would never have missed a Silver Taps ceremony or an Aggie Muster.

At 10:15 p.m., our family stood in an area cordoned off for relatives of Aggies being honored. We watched in silence as all the lights on the campus were extinguished and we were cast into darkness. In the next moment, the bell tower began playing hymns. As the music played, students—thousands of them—began gathering in silence in front of the Sul Ross statue. I trembled when a student came to usher our family into the assembly. Moments later, at precisely 10:30 p.m., Ross Volunteers marched over to the plaza and fired a 21-gun salute. Buglers began playing a special rendition of Taps, known as Silver Taps, playing it three times: once facing to the north, once to the south, and once to the west. Aggie Tradition dictates that taps is never played to the east because "the sun will never rise on that Aggie again."

The buglers finished their tribute and the students began walking away in silence. Awed, I watched and listened: so many people— and all we heard were the shuffling sounds of soft and careful footsteps and the nighttime chirping of cicadas.

As the crowd grew smaller, a fellow from the Corps of Cadets approached Tom and me and introduced himself. "I'm Mary's son, David's chemo nurse," he said.

Tom and I both choked on tears. Thinking of Mary and Derek and their tender care for David always triggered deep emotions in us. We didn't have words to tell this young freshman cadet how much it meant that he took time to introduce himself to us.

"My mom wanted to come, but she just couldn't get here," he added.

Oh, how I wished at that moment that I could see her again, tell her how much she meant to us, to David. I wanted to hug and thank her one more time.

The evening wasn't over yet. I recall the pain and agony that washed over me as Tom and I moved slowly, sadly, toward the Memorial Student Center where students waited to greet us and pay their respects. I couldn't control my thoughts.

Why us, God? Why David? How can I ever get beyond the pain of his absence?

Looking around at the crowd of vibrant young people, so full of life and promise, I thought, *David should have been here. This is all wrong...*

I felt so broken.

As throngs of David's friends greeted us and paid their respects, I tried to focus on how much David was loved and respected. I felt comforted as, one by one, hundreds of students, milling around and visiting, stopped to hug us or share a kind word. It was after midnight before the last words were said and the building was empty. Exhausted, but grateful, we walked the few steps to the hotel room upstairs in the MSC.

I thought, *I will never forget this night.*

It had been an amazing tribute—the darkened campus, all lights extinguished, the sound of Taps, the soft movements of so many who gathered to honor and remember. I felt honored, valued by the vast Aggie community, but nothing could displace my feelings of sadness and brokenness. I missed David desperately.

I grabbed onto the thought that I was not alone. God was with me in my sadness. And Tom and Andrew and Jon and Stephanie—together we would remember this night, and together we would continue to learn how to live with our grief.

* * *

Tom's reflections, early September, 2005

This morning I wake up sad, feeling incapacitated for the first time. I don't want to get out of bed. I don't want to go back to work. I feel depleted. I've never felt this way before.

Silver Taps drained me. I am glad it is behind us. The quietness and darkness of the moment, other than the 21 gun salute which startled me with its loudness, seemed to mirror my grief. I am quietly hurting and not seeing much light in my life.

I am thankful, though, for the way the whole campus honored David, and other current Aggies who have died. As a family, all of us have learned to love A&M—its people and its traditions. The school left an indelible imprint on David and Jon. It has left its imprint on me as well. I feel great appreciation and respect, but it is not enough to displace the deep sadness in my heart this morning.

The sadness permeates everything. Laura and I are struggling—I never expected that we would move forward (or backwards) with our healing in such a dissimilar manner. Maybe it's simply a male/female dysfunction, but the strain on our relationship is real and biting. Clearly we're not walking in lockstep with each other as we grieve. It is easy to feel resentment toward each other due to the dissimilarities. I wonder: due to our different personalities, is our uneven progress more difficult than other couples experience?

It's not like me to still be in bed this morning, at this hour. Jon has left for work and Andrew for school. My sons are facing the world and meeting their responsibilities, but I am struggling to get up.

If they can do it, I can too.

Thank you, Lord, for their strength and example.

CHAPTER 21

On an early October morning, exactly one month after the Silver Taps ceremony at Texas A&M, my friend Trina phoned me. I was surprised to hear her voice. Although our friendship went back fifteen years, our lives connected through our children and we hadn't spoken since before David's death. She asked if she could come visit; she had something special to share with me. Trina arrived at my front door moments later, excitedly holding a scrap of paper.

"I woke up at 5:00 this morning, remembering a vivid dream I had last night about your precious David. It's only the second time I've ever vividly recalled a dream," she said as we sat down together on my living room sofa. She smoothed out the wrinkled paper she had clutched as she drove over. "I didn't want to forget it so I wrote it down immediately."

She began reading aloud to me.

"How handsome and radiant he looked. He walked up to me and gave me a huge hug and asked if he could show me where he was and what he was doing. As he walked he told me, 'Aunt Trina, in heaven the greens are greener and the goals are higher.' As he said these things I saw a beautiful golf course, one hundred times prettier than Pebble Beach. Then we walked through a huge valley where a basketball court appeared in a great white light. It had a very tall post—the size of a telephone pole—and it was made of gold. David then asked if I wanted to see his house in heaven. He took me through a beautiful valley and into a forest. A huge house appeared, gorgeous and splendid. Surrounding the whole house was a porch with many rocking chairs all filled with people. He said, 'All these people are my family and we are doing what God created us to do, worshipping and praising Him!' All ages and sexes greeted me on the backyard lawn. We were overlooking a beautiful lake. David said, 'Here is where I live, and God is giving me the desires of my heart.' Then he added, 'Please tell my mom that I am happy and doing all the desires of my heart.'"

As Trina read, I began crying and shaking.

How could she have known? I wondered.

For weeks I had been reading every book on heaven that I could get my hands on. My hunger to know what life was like for David was insatiable. What was he doing? Was he enjoying any of the familiar things that brought him joy during his life here with us? As I finished reading one book, friends recommended another, and I searched each one intently. I begged God daily, with fervent tears, to give me a revelation, some glimpse, into this special place where my son was living. I missed him so.

Now, here beside me was my friend, sent in answer to my prayers. Trina and I shared the awesome realization of what God had done for me through her.

"I awoke from that dream with an urgent need to tell you about David's message," Trina said, wiping at her own tears. "God continued to impress upon me in my quiet time to go see you today. I believe He wants you to know that David is happy and doing all that God created him to do and be for His kingdom."

Overwhelmed by peace at that moment, I felt rest enter my soul, and comfort. My desperate prayer had been answered, and I would be forever grateful. Over and over I replayed David's message to me: *Please tell my Mom that I am happy and doing ALL the desires of my heart.*

It was more than I had asked for, more than I could have imagined.

When my choking tears subsided I told Trina how timely her visit was.

"I'm not surprised he called you 'Aunt Trina,'" I said, "He always adored and respected you. He's known you most of his life."

We laughed, remembering some of his childhood antics.

I shook my head, amazed. "How wonderful that he is continuing to play basketball and golf—two of his passions—and in such majestic and splendid surroundings! David loved water, whether it was a lake or the ocean."

Please tell my mom... The words continued to resonate in my soul, and I felt enveloped by the goodness and compassion of God.

That day I took another step toward hope amidst the shadows of grief. For a mom to know her son is praising and worshipping God, *in His presence,* and in perfect bliss—it brought a quiet sense of peace into the depths of my heart.

It was only the beginning, it seemed. In the weeks that followed, every time I needed a glimpse of God's greater purpose in the midst of my suffering, He revealed something. I began learning to open my eyes to see the unique ways His gentle care came to me, through my friends and through my circumstances.

I was able to think back to other moments of gentleness—those times when, unbeknownst to me, God had cared for me, sheltering me beneath the wings of His abiding care, sheltering me from knowledge that I was not yet able to bear. I saw how, almost imperceptibly, God had prepared me for the moment when He chose to reveal to me, and to Tom, the truth that David would not survive. In full view of his desperate illness and the extreme medical procedures, it had to be nothing less than the provision of immense grace that enabled us to trust and carry on, our minds sheltered from the truth that we were not yet capable of enduring.

The same month that I learned of Trina's special dream, God delivered another powerful message, a message that carried a strong sense of the supernatural—something Tom and I had never experienced before.

We had left town for a change of scenery with our friends, Brenda and Tyler. Feeling raw and emotionally beaten down, we traveled to the southern coast of California to enjoy the beauty of the ocean and the beach for a few days.

The day we arrived, October 17th, a sudden rain storm drove us to take cover in Ruby's Diner, a small restaurant on the pier. As we were leaving, a young couple approached us and began a conversation with us. We introduced ourselves and learned that the young man, Chris, spent his days ministering to people on the beach. The conversation was short, not even ten minutes, but it quickly turned meaningful.

"You have had a crisis in your lives," he said, pausing to glance at all of us.

Startled, I answered, "Yes, our son died, just four months ago."

"I'm sorry, so very sorry," Chris said.

I told him about David's lymphoma, about his courageous battle for life. Tears began as we shared David's story, Brenda and Tyler adding their memories and feelings. I was weeping and struggling for control.

Chris continued to look at me. "Are you writing or journaling, Laura?"

Tom and I exchanged baffled looks. I answered, "Yes, I write in a personal journal, but only to help me with the grief process. It's always helped me to put my thoughts on paper."

Chris stepped a little closer. "I feel you should continue to write," he said. "You have a story to share with others."

I glanced again at Tom.

"Would it be okay if I prayed for you?" Chris asked.

When I agreed, he put his hand on my shoulder, huddled us together and began praying for the Spirit's work in the writing of the story to be shared.

At the end of his prayer, he put his hand to his throat and said, "Someone in your family has a throat problem."

"No, no, not throat. It was David's lungs. He died from chemo complications that damaged his lungs," I told him.

"No," Chris answered emphatically. His hand still on his throat, he repeated, "Someone close to you has a throat problem."

We looked at each other, puzzled. None of us felt ill. Not one of us had mentioned a sore throat, or any other discomfort. I began to wonder: Was Chris God's minister, or was he a charlatan? Was there any truth in his words, or was he a deceiver? His friendliness and compassion were palpable, and he had discerned things about us that he couldn't have known apart from something supernatural at work, but doubt mingled with my desire to believe. I felt curious, intrigued, if a little skeptical.

Time will tell, I thought.

In the next moment, the sun broke through the clouds and we all began moving toward the door. Chris made another statement addressing Tom. We wondered about it as well. He then walked with us onto the boardwalk, and as we parted to go our separate ways, I said, "Thank you for praying for us. Would you keep praying for us, and for our other sons, Jon and Andrew?"

Whatever the outcome of his predictions, I felt Chris had a caring heart, a heart for prayer. I walked away comforted by that, and decided to write down all he had said. I would wait to see what happened next.

The day Brenda and Tyler returned home, their daughter Megan called and asked them to get her an appointment with a throat specialist. She had a dangerously enlarged tonsil causing great pain. Hours later, they learned she needed an emergency tonsillectomy.

"It could be a bad case of tonsillitis, but honestly, I'm afraid it has all the characteristics of lymphoma," the doctor told Brenda and Tyler.

Stunned, our friends called us with the terrifying news. Lymphoma. The kind of lymphoma that killed David. We were all shocked and terrified. Chris's words came back as a kind of haunting. Had God given him a message to prepare us all for the worst possible news a parent can receive?

Days of prayer followed the emergency tonsillectomy—prayer vigils held at our church, many friends enlisted to pray, as we all waited for the results of the biopsy. When we learned the tonsil was benign, it was hard not to wonder if Megan had truly had lymphoma. Had God chosen to heal her in response to the prayers of many? I wondered: would God have given us a message from a stranger on the beach if there really were no emergency, no urgent reason for prayer?

How could Chris have known? I wondered, pondering the way circumstances and situations were unfolding before me.

I thought about all he had said. *Write your story...share your story...*

Anxiety gripped me. I couldn't imagine traveling back through the pages of my journal, rereading the pain and fear, reliving the horror of watching David suffer and die, and then sharing my private agony with others.

I write because I have to, I told myself. *I write because I hope God will heal me as I open my heart to Him with pen and paper.*

Writing for any other purpose seemed impossible to me. Everything that was asked of me, every chore, even the most basics of family care, demanded more of me than I had to give. Yet, I seemed unable to forget Chris's words to me.

At times, I was able to meditate on the truth of God's sovereignty. I could trust Him to be in control of all things, I knew. I continued to wonder: Had He really chosen us to receive a special message from a stranger with a gift of foreknowledge? I didn't want to limit God by my imagination or my experiences. I wanted to embrace the possibility that Chris's words were actually a message from God. I couldn't dismiss what he said. But neither could I begin to act on it.

I felt depleted. My life was a dark tunnel. I could see no light ahead. The moments of greatest comfort came as I thought about Trina's dream. I could imagine David in that magnificent place—a real, literal place—with our Lord, doing all the things that brought him delight, fully experiencing the desires of his heart. I felt incredible peace and joy in those moments, but the times between were horrific.

Tom and I were upside down with grief as we thought about having to go through the upcoming holidays without Dave. If we were going to survive Thanksgiving and Christmas without David, we would have to muster all our strength. It wouldn't be enough—not our strength alone; we would need strength beyond our own. We would need God to come through for us in ways beyond our knowing.

As the days passed and holiday decorations began to appear all around me, I struggled to endure my heart's aching. One day, as the pain seemed to reach a crescendo, I heard Beth Moore's words on a local radio show:

"When our hearts are hemorrhaging with grief and loss,
never forget that Christ binds and compresses it
with a nail-scarred hand…
Christ never allows the hearts of his own
to be shattered without excellent reasons and eternal purposes."

So, Christ purposely allowed us to suffer this deep loss—I tried to wrap my brain around that thought—not for the first time since stepping on this road of grief. I had to walk by faith, one footstep at a time, asking God to help me believe the best about Christ. In all his suffering, David kept on believing in the beauty and goodness of his God. How did he do it? I wondered. Could I learn to do it, too?

Could I, like David, trust Jesus to carry me through my pain, meditating on the beauty of His attributes, trusting that He would one day heal me? Could I believe, and keep on believing, that God's great and glorious purposes were fulfilled in taking David from us? Could I believe that God would carry out to completion His purposes in my life? In Tom's? In Jon's and Andrew's?

I had more questions than answers, but I wanted to believe. I wanted to trust and be healed and feel whole again. I truly did want to believe the best about Christ. Together, Tom and I made that our prayer: that we would be able to see God's beauty and goodness, in spite of our loss; that we might someday receive glimpses of God's "excellent reason" for shattering our hearts, and learn to be at peace with His eternal purposes.

***

Tom's reflections, November 2005

Grieving is tiring and difficult. It is also perplexing.

I have renewed my work schedule and routine. It still seems uncomfortable, but I have no choice. I should work, and I need to work. A few days ago, I was visiting with two partners and I laughed at a story. I immediately felt guilty that I had laughed and quietly returned to my office. I felt odd. What had I done wrong? Am I not supposed to feel humor or laughter now? A bit confused, I determine I have done nothing wrong—it is all right to laugh. But I wonder, what would others think of me? Have Laura, Jon or Andrew felt this unexpected reaction?

During the day, friends and business associates say hello, smile and briefly visit. Do they know I don't mind talking about David and what has happened? I want to talk about David but everyone thinks that one would not want to talk about his loved one. Another confusing arrangement.

The encounter with Chris in Newport Beach baffles me. I have evaluated the conversation over and over, scrutinizing its possible meaning. Who is that guy? Does he have the gift of foreknowledge?

It seems too unlikely of an event, but God does place people in our lives for specific reasons. If God ordained the encounter, what then does the Holy Spirit want to teach us or guide us toward?

And Laura is supposed to write a book about our family's journey with cancer? How would Laura muster the energy and clarity at this time to even start writing a book? How would anyone have the energy and desire to write a book this close to the death of a child? This does not make sense.

---

[1]Beth Moore, *Breaking Free, the Workbook* (Houston, Texas: Living Proof Ministries), 122

CHAPTER 22

Chris told me to share David's story. In the months after that encounter, the idea of writing and telling about all that David and our family had endured, was unfathomable. Even though grace and goodness permeated the story, I couldn't bring myself to sit down and write it. And yet, some small seed had been planted. While I couldn't begin to summon the strength to relive it and shape it for someone else to read, I couldn't dismiss the idea completely. I found myself pondering, wondering. Could I really do it? If not now, someday?

Someday, when I wasn't paralyzed with grief. Someday, when life wasn't unbearable with sadness too deep for words.

While Tom and the boys, carrying their own sadness, returned to work and school and new beginnings, I was stuck in a dangerous place, alone with my grief and unable to move forward, unable to move in any direction. Unable to do much more than think and grieve and question. It was time for me to get help. I made an appointment with a grief counselor named Lisa, hoping she could help me find a way back into life.

Laura, you've been grieving for your husband's loss, for your sons' losses. You've been grieving their pain, but not your own. It's time to do that now. It's time to grieve for yourself, for all *you've* lost," Lisa told me.

She was right. The multiplied burden of grief carried by the men I so deeply loved had embedded itself in my soul. I was struggling under the weight of their sadness, never taking time to grieve my own. Now it was time. Week after week, Lisa guided me in the hard work of mourning.

In the meantime, I struggled to continue to journal, writing the passages of grief. I looked back at my notes often, tracing the emotions, the rollercoaster ride of mourning, glimpsing hope on one page, despair on another. But always, I kept writing, chronicling the journey; always I kept looking back, re-reading, discovering tiny moments of joy tucked into the pages like forgotten bookmarks.

Maybe, I thought. *Maybe one day I will write about David's battle, when the vibrant colors of his memory are not shaded by the impenetrable darkness of grief.*

In the fall of 2007, nearly two years after meeting Chris, I read *Same Kind of Different As Me,* written by Ron Hall and Denver Moore. I was inspired by the incredible story of these two men, one an art dealer and the other a modern day slave. Their eloquent telling seemed to call out to something deep inside me. I recognized it as the increasing desire to write David's story. A year later, when I had the chance to meet them at a book launch Ron Hall was hosting for a friend, I was eager to go. It was not only a chance to meet three very interesting people but also a chance to glean wisdom from them to begin writing my story.

On the day of the event, I was thrilled. When Tom called from the office complaining of flu-like symptoms, saying he couldn't go, I was crushed. It was an invitation only, private gathering. I could not call a friend to attend in Tom's place.

"I think you should go on without me," Tom insisted, when I fussed at him to change his mind.

I debated, wanting desperately to attend, sensing something momentous awaited me that night. Something I couldn't risk missing. I was right. The moment I entered the house, I knew this evening was going to be unlike any other social event I had ever attended.

I enjoyed meeting the host and author, Ron Hall, and Karen James, his friend whose book was the occasion for the gathering. While they greeted guests, I began circulating, hoping for a chance to speak privately with Denver. I found him visiting in the dining room, wearing his hat and looking dapper. I worked my way through the crowd and introduced myself.

For ten minutes we talked about his book, about the way it had come about, and the amazing story of his life. I told him how his writing, as well as Ron's, was an inspiration to me, and how I felt it might be time to tell my story, David's story. I described the pain of losing our son, and I told him about the message from Chris.

Denver leaned toward me. "Don't hide your pearls, Miss Laura," he said with richly accented words. "The pearl is like Christ—pure and reflective." His breath was very close to my face. "Don't dwell on your tragedy, for the Lord gives and the Lord takes away. We are told to be fishers of men! What are you waiting for? You have a job to do, so start writing your story!"

That night, December 3, 2008, was a night of profound spiritual impact. I went home with Denver's words ringing in my heart. It was the boost of confidence I needed. I knew a painful journey lay ahead for me, but I knew, with a new certainty, that God would partner with me. When I shared with Tom the strong urgings I felt about writing, he agreed to partner with me, as well. We determined, together, to tell our family's story. It was time.

In the weeks that followed, I recalled Denver's words about pearls. I laid them out on my night stand, twirled them as I browsed my journal, looking back at where we had been, noticing encounters with joy, moments of bliss sprinkled across the landscape of grief. I read my journal entry from New Year's Eve, 2006, when Jon married Stephanie. The ceremony was sweet and tender, and I saw how God enabled me to be fully engaged in the celebration of their marriage, even though my soul was still raw with sorrow. I turned the pages to read the account of Andrew's high school graduation a few months later, and again, I saw shimmers of pleasure.

I felt my chest constrict with pain as I read the entry of our trip to Pebble Beach in 2007—Andrew's choice for his graduation celebration. We returned to the magnificent course that meandered along the ocean—the place where we had celebrated David's graduation four years earlier, the course David loved. My heart ached as I read my own words, describing the beauty, noting David's absence. He seemed to be ever-present, and yet nowhere to be found. I saw the tear stains on the pages and wept with the yearning of a mother for her child. I wept for the complexity of life—the desperate desire for the freedom to celebrate for one son while bound to grief for another.

My pearls dangling around my neck, I read page after page, noticing that there is no symmetry to the life of a grieving parent. At one moment, it tilts off-balance toward a fearful fall into complete despair. At another, it slides almost unwillingly toward joy and hope. There is no predicting which way it will lean.

Reading, re-reading, I began to discern this truth: There is no pattern for mourning; it is random; it is complex.

There is no right way, no wrong way, to experience grief.

I understood, finally, that there is no right way, *no wrong way to begin writing about it.*

There is simply this: Begin.

"Begin," Chris told me.

"Begin," Denver said.

Lisa's voice chimed in one day at the close of my counseling session.

"Laura, I see in you a peace and contentment I've never seen before. I've never said this to a client, but you have a story to share. Open your journal and begin writing."

Four years after David's death, I sat down to write his story to share with others.

I knew I wanted God to be glorified and in so doing, David would be remembered.

My hands on the keyboard, the story unfolding, I stared at the chronology of events, startled at the realization that I was given one sacred year to care for David. For hours at a time, I read through my journal. Little did I realize in 2004, when I was writing about David, that it would be my last year with him; my last year with my family as it had always been, as I had always believed it would be.

Had things happened differently I might not have had even that *one* last year. The thought captivated me as I read and re-read the events of that year.

So many variables could have caused a different outcome. Tom and I came to realize that David, or one or both of the girls riding in the vehicle with him, could have been killed in the rollover accident. (One of the girls had just unbuckled her seat belt before the accident.) The paramedics on the scene heard David's cough and thought it was bad enough to warrant chest x-rays. The ER physician, Dr. Goodman, after studying the films, emphatically urged us to have David examined by an oncologist as soon as he was released to travel home to Arlington. Hours later, David was in Dr. Firstenberg's office, and we were hearing the words "cancer" and "aggressive lymphoma", and wondering how our orderly suburban lives could have taken such a sudden turn into confusion and terror.

"This is a cancer that moves very quickly," Dr. F told us.

Typing the notes from my journal into my computer, I realized, maybe for the first time, that David's life might have ended much sooner. I shuddered as I thought of how easily I could have continued trying to treat David's cough, thinking he had bronchitis, never imagining that a cancerous mass close to his aorta was growing unseen, unknown. It was true: the accident that could have ended his life gave him another year with us. One last sacred year.

Turning the pages of my journal, I recalled a phone call from Derek, David's nurse in Arlington, about a year after David's passing. He shared his memories of David, reflecting on his last months of life. He told me Mary, who also cared for David, left oncology soon after David died. I was surprised—she was passionate about her work—and I wondered at the toll such work might take on a gentle soul. I wished her well wherever she was.

Derek believed David knew when he left MD Anderson to return to Arlington that he wasn't going to win his battle against cancer. He knew his fight was coming to an end.

"I could read it in his eyes," Derek told me. "They spoke peace and resolve. He was satisfied with his life; he was prepared."

Tears flowed, as they always did, when I read back over conversations like this—conversations I was so thankful to have recorded in my journal.

"David couldn't tell you these things," Derek said. "He was always concerned for you, for his family."

Once again, I felt such gratitude to God that He prompted Tom and me to go to David, in his last hours, while he was sedated, and speak our love for him, blessing him, assuring him we would be all right, and finally, letting him go.

In my journal that day I wrote, "David heard our words. I believe he was set free."

Folded and tucked among the pages of my journal I found a letter David's dear friend Courtni wrote to us after David died. Reading it, I found myself laughing at the way David charmed her parents when he met them for the first time, the way he made them laugh.

"There's something different about that fellow," they told Courtni, after spending an evening with David.

"David captivated them," Courtni wrote. "His laughter, his love of life—they were drawn to him."

Her letter described the day she went to watch an intramural basketball game at a gym at Texas A&M. The team David played on was on the court, huddled before the tip-off. David was in the middle, surrounded by his teammates, also his closest friends. He couldn't play—he had relapsed. His cancer had returned and he had a port in his chest, but he showed up wearing his yellow jersey, pumped and ready to cheer on his friends. When the huddle broke, David joined Courtni in the stands.

She wrote:

Cheering each one of his friends on, motivated by his love for them and his competitive spirit, he was no less part of the team on the sidelines than on the court. Each huddle, I watched him slowly walk over to the guys, throw his hand on top of the others and give his whole heart in encouraging them. Tears filled my eyes time after time, thinking about how badly he wanted to be out there, running, having fun with the guys, just doing what he was so great at—play! Though his body kept him from doing so, his heart was all there. I was so encouraged when I left that game: encouraged to live each moment fully and without restraint; to truly live as if there is no tomorrow. To live like David lived.

I paused from reading, letting myself remember the joy of watching David at play. Courtni was right—"play" was one of the things David did best. Whether it was basketball, golf, puzzles—whatever he picked up to do, he could make it fun. His playfulness was one of his greatest gifts. I let myself say thank-you to God, and to Courtni, for this sweet reminder.

I continued reading:

One of my favorite date parties with David was the Chi-O formal the spring semester of our freshman year. He was on a mission to find the perfect tie, a pink one to match my dress, and he succeeded. We were the most coordinated couple at the formal! I had so much fun with him—a wonderful dinner, then Blackjack at the casino, and then dancing like crazy. The best part of the night was the final song, "With You", by Jessica Simpson. I've never seen a guy so excited to hear a song. I watched with amazement as David completely let loose and belted every single word. I remember thinking, "I have the coolest date here!" He made the night such a blast and made me feel like a million bucks. He made everyone feel like that. It was this kind of carefree experience with David that I loved. I loved being around someone who was not ashamed to dance, to live fully. Your son's life deeply impacted me, and there are many more incredible memories of him etched deeply in my heart.

I put the letter down and closed my eyes. I let myself remember David on the dance floor. I saw his lanky body moving as though boneless, uninhibited, fueled by the pure joy of life. I chuckled. How I missed him. And yet, there I sat, smiling, thinking of the pleasure he brought to our lives. I returned to the letter:

I saw David for the last time just before he had to return to MD Anderson. He was starting chemo treatments again. I asked him for one thing that I could specifically pray about for him. His eyes welled up with tears and he said, "Honestly, Courtni, please pray for my family. They have been through so much, especially my mom. I know it will be hard on her being in Houston. So I would love it if you would pray for them more than anything. Not me—pray for my family." He was worried about the burden of his illness. I assured him that you loved caring for him. As a mother, no greater joy could have been brought to your heart than spending time with him, no matter what that meant. I went to my knees for the Gilbert family, for your hearts to be at rest.

Many letters came in the months and even years after David's death, but the message of this one settled deep into my heart. I knew these were words I would treasure.

I continued to peruse my journal, thumbing through my own writings, and I found several accounts of Courtni's visits in our home. I sat for several minutes, remembering laughter and good times.

Over the next several months, as I re-read my words, and rewrote them, I discerned many things. I saw clearly that mourning is a random thing, yes, but I noticed that, for me, it had an odd kind of symmetry to it. It seemed as though for every paragraph that contained sorrow and grief, there was another that spoke of God's tenderness, His kindness toward me, toward my family. For every sorrow, I read a comfort and a promise of help.

Some entries were poignant with the blend of joy and sadness. Mother's Day would always be difficult, I thought.

And Father's Day, for Tom. Would he ever be free of the memory that David's visitation at the funeral home was held on that day?

And yet, as I read, I saw that we continued to go through the motions of living. We continued to put one foot in front of the other—even though at times that itself had seemed almost impossible. We did it for our other sons, Jon and Andrew. We did it for each other, Tom and I. And we did it for ourselves, I suspect, because for all our sadness, we knew life is a gift, and we mustn't squander it. Of all the things David taught us, perhaps that was his greatest lesson to us.

On some pages, I read about good times, laughter, sweet moments with Andrew, Jon and Stephanie, as well as accounts of meaningful experiences with friends and other family members.

On every page I read about the journey of faith and discovery.

I read of rainbows and dreams of heaven and sweet messages that delivered hope and peace. I re-read Chris's words, letters from David's friends; I read countless provisions of God's grace, sometimes brought by His people, sometimes brought by a scripture passage; grace sometimes seen in nothing more than the presence of a bird on my balcony railing.

With each page I re-read, and each page I typed, I saw that joy was a continuous surprise; that life was good; that there was pleasure to be experienced, hope to be expressed and fun to be had.

David loved to sing in the shower, he danced like no one was watching; he laughed loudly and often. His practical jokes and his freewheeling style of humor were surprising and fun. He lived out his passion and his faith.

I remembered how he loved the phrase: Carpe Diem!

Seize the day!

It was how he lived his life. It was how I wanted to live my life.

Reaching for my pen and journal, I penned the words, "Carpe Diem, David."

And then I added, "I am satisfied."

EPILOGUE

Today, July 16, 2011, would have been David's 27th birthday. Six years have passed since his death.

Tonight I will dance with my husband at our niece Laura's wedding. It is what David would have wanted. For this date to be forever matched with love and music and good times—David would have been thrilled. When Tom and I step onto the dance floor, it will be David we are thinking of: remembering his birth, his life, his irreplaceable presence in our hearts, in our family.

We will share the dance floor with many—including Jon, Stephanie and Andrew. We will toast the joy of Laura and John's marriage, and we will raise our hearts in gratitude to God for the life of our son David. We will honor his memory every year as Laura and John mark this day as their anniversary, and it will be forever linked with the delight of laughter and gifts and music and dance.

It seems a fitting marker for the life David lived. It seems a fitting marker for the way I choose to live the rest of my life, without David.

In the seven years since that fateful phone call in the wee hours of the morning, I have experienced the kindness of friends and strangers alike. I have experienced God's patient nurturing of my soul as He walked with me through the darkest days a mother can endure.

On a recent radio broadcast, I heard Dr. James Dobson say, "A mother and a child have a special bond and there is nothing like it in the universe." I appreciate his words. They express a mother's love—so pure, tender, and protective. Upon the death of a child, a sacred physical bond is severed forever. The pain is deep and harsh beyond describing, yet it need not define us. It need not rob us of the capacity to live fully, richly, with abandonment to the pleasure of present joys and the hope of future grace.

As I write this, preparations are underway for the sixth annual Gilbert Leadership Conference. Tom and I continue to be amazed and humbled when we think about all the hard work and creative energies invested by David's friends to make this conference a reality. It is one of the answers to our daily prayer, asking God to give us glimpses into His higher purposes for taking David and to show us what our "new normal" without David should be.

In a few short months, our family will join student delegates in Houston where we have the opportunity to participate in the conference -- a four day leadership event that invites 32 freshman delegates from Texas A&M to gather together to focus on character, service and involvement. It is a conference that embodies the spirit of David, as seen and loved by his closest friends. It is my family's great honor and blessing to continue to be a part of it.

But first, a wedding. And a dance.

Today, anticipating the celebration we will attend on this, David's birthday, I think about Henri Nouwen's words to those of us who mourn:

> "Mourning makes us poor; it powerfully reminds us of our smallness. But it is precisely here, in that pain or poverty or awkwardness that the Dancer invites us to rise up and take the first steps. For in our suffering, not apart, Jesus enters our sadness, takes us by the hand, pulls us gently up to stand, and invites us to dance. We find the way to pray, as the psalmist did, 'You have turned my mourning into dancing' (Psalm 30:11), because at the center of our grief we find the grace of God...we come to know that all the world is our dance floor."

I feel drawn to the dance floor, the Dancer inviting me to move back into the rhythms of life. I'm not so naïve as to think I will always move with a light step—pain, quite often, is a mere breath away, and it quickly, easily drops me to my knees. Little things, often unexpected things, trigger the deep sense of loss, and I must mourn again. But I know I can live with both the pain and the pleasure. A burden has been lifted. I feel as though I have awakened to a new life. Even so, I expect my steps to be awkward—I am still in poverty; I am still in pain. But I have discovered the grace of God at the center of my grief. He's offering me His hand, inviting me to dance—but not as though no one is watching. Tonight, I'll dance as though David is watching. I'll dance to honor his enduring passion for life.

I'll dance, because to sit on the sidelines of life, watching, refusing to celebrate the sweetness of life would be an affront to the memory of David and the life he lived. It would mean I have learned nothing from the sacred year we shared.

So, I'll wear my pearls and dance with Tom, remembering, savoring, loving.

Happy birthday, David.

---

[1]Nouwen, Henry, *Turn My Mourning Into Dancing* (Nashville, TN: Word Publishing, 2001), 32

11887357R0011

Made in the USA
Lexington, KY
08 November 2011